The United Nations and Global Change

Herausgegeben von

Prof. Dr. Manuel Fröhlich,
Universität Jena

Dr. Andreas Rechkemmer,
United Nations University, UN Campus Bonn

Prof. Dr. Dr. Sabine von Schorlemer,
Technische Universität Dresden

Prof. Dr. Johannes Varwick,
Christian-Albrechts-Universität zu Kiel

Band 2

Dr. Ekkehard Strauss

The Emperor‘s New Clothes?

The United Nations and the implementation of the responsibility to protect

Nomos

Die Deutsche Nationalbibliothek verzeichnet diese Publikation in der Deutschen Nationalbibliografie; detaillierte bibliografische Daten sind im Internet über http://www.d-nb.de abrufbar.

Die Deutsche Nationalbibliothek lists this publication in the Deutsche Nationalbibliografie; detailed bibliographic data is available in the Internet at http://www.d-nb.de .

ISBN 978-3-8329-4392-9

1. Auflage 2009

Preface

An emperor who cared much about his appearance hired two tailors who promised him the finest garments from the most beautiful cloth. The modern fabric was invisible to anyone stupid or unfit for his position, the two swindlers told the king. Neither the emperor nor his ministers could see the non-existing clothes when they were invited to the tailors' fitting room, but pretended that they could for fear of being considered stupid. When the swindlers reported that the suit was finished, they dressed the emperor in mime. The king presented his new clothes during a procession through the capital. When a child cried out that the king, in fact, was naked, the crowd realized it was telling the truth. The emperor, however, held his head high and continued the procession.

The fairy tale by Hans-Christian Andersen could be a metaphor for the main arguments currently exchanged on the operationalization of the responsibility to protect within the United Nations. According to some, the responsibility to protect does not add anything to existing international obligations and practice. Without addressing the real causes for inaction in cases of genocide, war crimes, ethnic cleansing and crimes against humanity, in particular the membership and veto power in the Security Council, the United Nations would remain naked in the face of future challenges. Others argue that while presented as a new dress, the responsibility to protect only provides another justification for so called humanitarian interventions of powerful governments, sometimes on behalf of the United Nations, in the internal affairs of weak Member States. A third group seeks to build on the limited agreement reflected in the Summit Outcome document and to explore ways to implement it. This group is divided between those, who advocate an extensive interpretation of the agreement, and others, who would prefer promoting a case-by-case application based on a common denominator which does not require agreement on all details of the interpretation of the Outcome Document.

This publication attempts to assist the ongoing discussion on the operationalization of the responsibility to protect by the United Nations. After summarizing the negotiation process towards the agreement in the Summit Outcome document, the practice of the application of the responsibility to protect by United Nations organs and other bodies since September 2005 is presented, before providing elements for a comprehensive review of existing United Nations capacities to prevent or halt genocide, war crimes, ethnic cleansing and crimes against humanity. Finally, the publication proposes elements for an immediate strategy of the Secretary-General and the United Nations departments, funds and agencies to facilitate the application of the responsibility to protect in practice in the immediate future.

While mainly addressed to policy practitioners within the United Nations, Member States and civil society, hopefully, much of the content of the present publication will provide some initial reference for future in-depth academic review of the many historic, legal, military and other issues closely related to the implementation of the responsibility to protect.

The main part of this study was prepared during a sabbatical leave generously granted to me by the United Nations Secretariat during the summer of 2008. I am most grateful to the New York Office of the High Commissioner for Human Rights for the support of my participation in the programme. Without the invitation by Professor Sabine von Schorlemer and the Faculty of Law of the Technical University of Dresden to provide office space and academic support, this project could not have been realized. In addition, many colleagues at the United Nations, Permanent Missions, national governments, civil society and academia took the time to share their knowledge and experience.

New York, October 2008

Contents

A. The revival of the bell-bottoms? - The Responsibility to Protect deconstructed

1. The responsibility to protect at the 2005 World Summit

On 14 September 2005, Secretary-General Kofi Annan addressed the largest gathering of world leaders in the history of the United Nations in the General Assembly hall at the United Nations Headquarters in New York.[1] Opening the three-day meeting known as the 2005 World Summit, he summarized the negotiations towards the meeting and the main agreement of the Member States, including the following paragraph:

> 'For the first time, you will accept, clearly and unambiguously, that you have a collective responsibility to protect populations from genocide, war crimes, ethnic cleansing and crimes against humanity. You will make clear your willingness to take timely and decisive collective action through the Security Council, when peaceful means prove inadequate and national authorities are manifestly failing to protect their own populations. Excellencies, you will be pledged to act if another Rwanda looms.'

This statement was remarkable for both its certainty of the interpretation of the agreement and the optimism regarding its future implementation. The outgoing Secretary-General considered an agreement on the responsibility to protect a core area of the Summit Outcome document. With a view to the experience in Rwanda and Srebrenica, he felt that the credibility of the United Nations and the principles of the Charter required clear guidance to the Member States, how to engage in similar situations in the future. At the end of his tenure, he wanted to witness the transition from principle to operational action. Only hours before Heads of State and Government arrived in New York for their gathering, it looked as if no final document would be available for their signature, when negotiations stalled on main parts of the agreement, including the responsibility to protect.

When Canada initially proposed to include the responsibility to protect in the Outcome Document, the delegation chose to link the responsibility to protect with considerations on human security. This line of argument raised immediate concerns with some Member States. The concept of human security has been defined as the protection of "the vital core of all human lives in ways that enhance human freedoms and fulfillment."[2] It encompasses human rights, good governance and

1 See for details on the Summit http://www.un.org/summit2005/

2 *Human Security Center*, Human Security Report 2005. War and Peace in the 21st Century, University of British Colombia, Canada, 2005.

access to economic opportunity, education and health care.[3] Human security complements state security, enhances human rights and strengthens human development. It seeks to protect people against a broad range of threats to individuals and communities and, further, to empower them to act on their own behalf.[4]

The initial concerns of some Member States were reinforced when the draft Outcome Document of 3 June 2005 submitted by the President of the General Assembly, Jean Ping, included the responsibility to protect in a section on human rights and rule of law together with human security and the strengthening of the Office of the High Commissioner for Human Rights (OHCHR). The draft read as follows:

> 72. We agree that the responsibility to protect civilian populations lies first and foremost with each individual State. The international community should, as necessary, encourage and help States to exercise this responsibility. The international community has also the responsibility to use diplomatic, humanitarian and other peaceful means under Chapter VI and VIII of the UN Charter to help protect civilian populations from genocide, war crimes, ethnic cleansing, and crimes against humanity. If such peaceful means appear insufficient, we recognize our shared responsibility to take collective action, through the Security Council and, as appropriate, in cooperation with relevant regional organizations under Chapter VII of the Charter.
>
> 73. We support the implementation of the United Nations Action Plan to prevent genocide.
>
> 74. We stress the need to continue consideration of the concept of the responsibility to protect within the General Assembly.[5]

Initially, the draft paragraphs on the responsibility to protect were not very prominent in the negotiations. Security Council expansion was the first priority for Member States and other initiatives considered in a broader context of cooperation on the main issues. The responsibility to protect was perceived mainly as an interest of Canada, the European Union and Japan. Initially, the United States did not consider it a priority.[6] Thus, Member States assumed that a rejection could pay to get concessions in other areas of the document. It was expected that, ultimately, Russia would succeed in convincing the supporters to take the provisions out of the text. The main substantive concern regarding an agreement on the responsibility to protect was related to the principle of sovereignty and non-intervention. Another concern that was raised with some frequency was unilateral action under the auspices of the responsibility to protect. While Libya, Pakistan and Venezuela

3 *United Nations Development Programme*, Human Development Report 1994. New Dimensions of Human Security, Oxford University Press, 1994.

4 *Neil MacFarlane/ Yuen Foong Khong*, Human Security and the UN: A Critical History, Indiana University Press, 2006.

5 Draft Outcome Document by the President of the General Assembly of 3 June 2005, available at http://www.responsibilitytoprotect.org/index.php/united_nations/

6 Strong support came from the *Task Force on the United Nations*, American Interests and UN Reform, United States Institute for Peace, Washington D.C., 2005, p. 27 et seq.

pointed at their particular historic experience with interventions by foreign governments, other Member States, such as Belarus, China, Egypt, India, Iran and Jamaica, voiced their opposition in more general terms. The African countries broadly supported the idea, pointing at a similar provision in the Charter of the African Union.[7] The structure of the negotiations by main clusters, i.e. human rights, peace and security and development, forced the heads of delegation to focus on the most important questions related to peace and security, institutional reform and the guiding principles of the document leaving their experts with little guidance for furthering the discussion on the responsibility to protect. At the end of July, following the discussions among Member States, Ping presented an amended draft Document, including the following provisions on the responsibility to protect:

> 113. We agree that the responsibility to protect civilian populations lies first and foremost with each individual State and we accept that responsibility and agree to act in accordance with it. The international community should, as appropriate, encourage and help States to exercise this responsibility. The international community, through the United Nations, also has the responsibility to use diplomatic, humanitarian and other peaceful means, including under Chapters VI and VIII of the Charter to help protect civilian populations from genocide, war crimes, ethnic cleansing and crimes against humanity. In this context, we recognize our shared responsibility to take collective action, through the Security Council and, as appropriate, in cooperation with relevant regional arrangements, under Chapter VII of the Charter, should peaceful means proved insufficient and national authorities be unwilling or unable to protect their populations. We stress the need to continue consideration of the concept of the responsibility to protect within the sixtieth session of the General Assembly.
>
> 114. We support the implementation of the United Nations Action Plan to Prevent Genocide and the work of the Secretariat to this end.[8]

In their comments, Member States repeated their previous positions and it became clear that a consensus was difficult to extract. With a view to the importance of a successful Summit for the legacy of Kofi Annan and his particular interest, the Secretariat team around Assistant Secretary-General for Policy Coordination and Strategic Planning Bob Orr extended its mediation efforts between Member States on the responsibility to protect. In a marathon of meetings with Permanent Representatives they recalled the situations in Rwanda and Srebrenica and urged to put the joint interest of all Member States not to repeat previous failures into the center of attention.[9]

On 5 August, Jean Ping presented another revised draft Outcome Document. With regard to the responsibility to protect, the document introduced the limitation of the

7 See on the general political dynamics of the World Summit *Alex Bellamy*, Whither the Responsibility to Protect? Humanitarian Intervention and the 2005 World Summit, Ethics and International Affairs, Vol. 20, 2006, p. 151 et seq.

8 Revised draft outcome document of the high-level plenary meeting of the General Assembly of September 2005 submitted by the President of the General Assembly, U.N.-Doc. A/59/HPLM/CRP.1/Rev.1 of 22 July 2005.

9 See for details on the involvement of the Secretariat in the negotiations of the Summit Outcome document *James Traub*, The Best Intentions. Kofi Annan and the UN in the Era of American World Power, New York, 2006, p. 359 et seq., 373 et seq.

protection of populations from genocide, war crimes, ethnic cleansing and crimes against humanity. The Member States agreed that this responsibility to protect entailed the prevention of such crimes, including their incitement. They acknowledged that the international community, through the United Nations, also has the obligation - changed from "responsibility" - to use diplomatic, humanitarian and other peaceful means to help protect populations from these crimes. The revised text read as follows:

> 118. We agree that the protection of populations from genocide, war crimes, ethnic cleansing and crimes against humanity lies first and foremost with each individual State. We also agree that this responsibility to protect entails the prevention of such crimes, including their incitement. We accept this responsibility and agree to act in accordance with it. The international community should, as appropriate, encourage and help States to exercise this responsibility and support the efforts of the United Nations to establish an early-warning capability. The international community, through the United Nations, also has the obligation to use diplomatic, humanitarian and other peaceful means, including under Chapters VI and VIII of the Charter to help protect populations from genocide, war crimes, ethnic cleansing and crimes against humanity. In this context, we recognize our shared responsibility to take collective action, in a timely and decisive manner, through the Security Council under Chapter VII of the UN Charter and in co-operation with relevant regional organizations, should peaceful means be inadequate and national authorities be unwilling or unable to protect their populations. We stress the need to continue consideration of the concept of the responsibility to protect within the sixtieth session of the General Assembly.
>
> 119. We invite the permanent members of the Security Council to refrain from using the veto in cases of genocide, war crimes, ethnic cleansing and crimes against humanity.
>
> 120. We support the implementation of the United Nations Action Plan to Prevent Genocide and the work of the Secretariat to this end.[10]

On 17 August, the recently appointed Permanent Representative of the United States to the United Nations, Ambassador John Bolton, sent to his colleagues a list of amendments and changes to the draft document which had been negotiated for almost one year. While the United States had indicated earlier to accept most of the human rights and collective security agenda of the draft Document, many delegations had expected some development in the US position after a harsh rejection of the draft by the US delegation in the General Assembly two weeks earlier.[11] Initially, many Western countries appreciated the US initiative as they perceived the negotiations as giving in too much on development without getting back much on the responsibility to protect. However, only Algeria, Cuba, Egypt, Iran and Venezuela supported the idea of new negotiations publicly.

10 Revised draft outcome document of the high-level plenary meeting of the General Assembly of September 2005 submitted by the President of the General Assembly, U.N.-Doc. A/59/HPLM/CRP.1/Rev.2 of 5 August 2005.

11 Julian Borger, Road map for US relations with rest of world. Hundreds of deletions and insertions on just about every global issue could undermine the UN summit agreement, The Guardian, 27 August 2005.

The draft paragraph on the responsibility to protect was completely altered by the amendments, and the clause urging the five Permanent Members of the Security Council not to veto action aimed at halting or preventing genocide or ethnic cleansing was deleted. The United States requested, inter alia, to drop the reference to incitement and change the wording back to responsibility when describing the role of the international community. Ambassador Bolton explained further the position of the United States on the section on the responsibility to protect in the revised draft document in a letter dated 30 August 2005 and proposed the following wording:

> 118. We underscore that national authorities have a responsibility to protect their populations and, in cases involving genocide, ethnic cleansing crimes against humanity and other large-scale atrocities in which national authorities are unwilling or unable to protect their citizens. Then the international community should be prepared to use diplomatic, humanitarian, and other methods to protect civilian populations. And if such methods appear insufficient the Security Council may out of necessity decide to take action under the Charter, including enforcement action, if so required.[12]

The last-minute demands by the United States changed the dynamics of the negotiations significantly as other Member States felt encouraged to fall back on their previous positions perceived to have been dropped in the process. Russia, for example, expressed its general objections to any attempt of granting authority to intervene in cases of genocide. China also voiced general concern regarding the responsibility to protect.[13]

In order to save the Summit, Jean Ping appointed a core group of thirty Member States to work through Ambassador Bolton's list concentrating on the main issues.[14] This group was later replaced by a group of only 12 Member States. On 2 September, the core group reported that the sub-group on the responsibility to protect had two readings of the draft text, and despite efforts to reach agreement, fundamental differences remained. The group did succeed in identifying the most critical points of divergence since discussions had been more focused with individual delegations at the level of Ambassadors. However, when no progress was made with a harvest document drafted by the United Kingdom and 150 brackets remained to the draft Document, the Secretariat and Ping worked on a compromise text 24 hours before the heads of state arrived.

It is difficult to establish the details of the drama that unfolded subsequently in Conference Room 4 in the basement of the United Nations building in New York until the early hours of the day of the Summit as many witnesses cautiously try to align their records with their current interpretation of the Outcome Document. However, considering the varying accounts of participants in the light of the

12 US comments on the revised draft outcome document, A/59/HPLM/CRP.1/Rev.2, submitted on 17 August 2005 at 11.06 a.m.

13 On the background to Ambassador Bolton's initiative see Brian Urquhart, One Angry Man, New York Review of Books, 6 March 2008, p. 14.

14 Maggie Farley, U.S. Demands Spur Crisis Talks at U.N., Los Angeles Times, 27 August 2005

differences between the text of the final Outcome Document, the revised draft of 5 August and the statements of the Heads of State and Government at the Summit, some important elements of the discussions can be reconstructed.

Russia, India and Jamaica argued against including the paragraph on the responsibility to protect in the Outcome Document. They claimed that the Charter established all necessary standards to address situations of mass atrocities. Furthermore, the responsibility to protect was already part of the international standards on the protection of civilians and the positive obligations deriving from the right to life. Other countries questioned who could make the legal determination that a Member State was 'unwilling and unable' to protect their populations. With a view to the same wording in the Rome Statute on the International Criminal Court and the recent referral of the situation in Darfur to the Court,[15] many members of the Group of 77 were concerned that, based on a similar assessment, measures of regime change could be taken against the will of the government concerned. It was argued that for lack of common ground the paragraph should leave any definition for later and only describe the 'contours' of the responsibility. At the same time, the Member States could not agree on a particular mechanism for future discussions.

Consequently, the Draft Negotiated Outcome distributed on 12 September 2005 took all these concerns into consideration and arrived at the following wording in the Summit Outcome document:

> 138. Each individual State has the responsibility to protect its populations from genocide, war crimes, ethnic cleansing and crimes against humanity. This responsibility entails the prevention of such crimes, including their incitement, through appropriate and necessary means. We accept that responsibility and will act in accordance with it. The international community should, as appropriate, encourage and help States to exercise this responsibility and support the United Nations in establishing an early warning capability.
>
> 139. The international community, through the United Nations, also has the responsibility to use appropriate diplomatic, humanitarian and other peaceful means, in accordance with Chapters VI and VIII of the Charter, to help to protect populations from genocide, war crimes, ethnic cleansing and crimes against humanity. In this context, we are prepared to take collective action, in a timely and decisive manner, through the Security Council, in accordance with the Charter, including Chapter VII, on a case-by-case basis and in cooperation with relevant regional organizations as appropriate, should peaceful means be inadequate and national authorities are manifestly failing to protect their populations from genocide, war crimes, ethnic cleansing and crimes against humanity. We stress the need for the General Assembly to continue consideration of the responsibility to protect populations from genocide, war crimes, ethnic cleansing and crimes against humanity and its implications, bearing in mind the principles of the Charter and international law. We also intend to commit ourselves, as necessary and appropriate, to helping States build capacity to protect their populations from genocide, war crimes, ethnic cleansing and crimes against humanity and to assisting those which are under stress before crises and conflicts break out.

15 U.N.-Doc. S/RES/1593 (2005) of 31 March 2005.

140. We fully support the mission of the Special Adviser of the Secretary-General on the Prevention of Genocide.[16]

The length of the sentences and the many sub-clauses reveal the effort of including the diverse positions in a compromise version. The two paragraphs separate the responsibility of individual States and the responsibility of the international community. The latter requires that national authorities of a Member State are 'manifestly failing' to meet their responsibility. Compared with the previous criteria of States being 'unwilling and unable', this wording indicates the intention to base any assessment on evidence rather than on a judgment of motives. Furthermore, the responsibility to protect is not qualified further as either an emerging norm of international law or another obligation. The responsibility to prevent in paragraph 138 is mainly expressed as an appeal. Paragraph 139 shows the agreement on the application of non-military means, while the Member States could only agree on the application of non-consensual means on a case-by-case basis. The paragraph concludes with the general caveat of the need for the General Assembly to further consider the responsibility to protect without the specific timetable 'at its 60th Session'. The appeal to the permanent members of the Security Council regarding the exercise of their veto was not included.[17]

Even though the Summit Outcome document was adopted without a vote, the subsequent statements of Heads of State and Government indicated the divisions prevailing on the responsibility to protect. Prime Minister Paul Martin of Canada referred to the responsibility to protect as a 'powerful norm of international behavior' and he was 'proud that R2P has Canadian lineage, that it is now a principle for all the world'. He argued that the responsibility to protect stood for clear, multilaterally agreed criteria on what the international community should do when civilians are at risk. Iceland and Italy referred to the responsibility to protect as concept, respectively a principle, while Mauritius called it a 'norm of collective action' and Norway a 'duty to help'. Indonesia underlined the need for a consensus on the responsibility to protect and Switzerland called on Member States to make every effort to define together the criteria for its implementation. Fierce criticism came from President Hugo Chavez Frias of Venezuela, who called on Member States not to allow a handful of countries to try to reinterpret the principles of international law and to give way to doctrines like preemptive war and the 'so called responsibility to protect'. President Robert G. Mugabe of Zimbabwe warned that the responsibility to protect needed careful scrutiny in order to test the motives of its proponents.[18]

In an op-ed appearing in The Wall Street Journal at the end of September, Secretary-General Kofi Annan acknowledged that the Summit Outcome document

16 U.N.-Doc. A/RES/60/1 of 24 October 2005.

17 See for a more comprehensive analysis of the Summit Outcome document *Carsten Stahn*, Responsibility to Protect: Political Rhetoric or Emerging Legal Norm?, AJIL, Vol. 101, No. 1, p. 99 et seq.

18 All statements are available at http://www.un.org/webcast/summit2005/statements.html

was disappointing in part. However, he described as 'most precious' 'the acceptance by all members of their collective responsibility to protect civilian populations against genocide, war crimes and crimes against humanity through the Security Council when local authorities are failing'. 'I first advocated this in 1998, as the inescapable lesson of our failures in Bosnia and Rwanda' he wrote. 'I am glad to see it generally accepted at last – and I hope it will be acted upon when put to the test'.[19]

With this statement, the competition for the authentic interpretation of the Summit Outcome document was opened.

More than three years after the Summit the competition is still employing various tools of advocacy. However, progress in the practical application of the responsibility to protect on country situations perceived as at risk regarding genocide, war crimes, ethnic cleansing or crimes against humanity could hardly be observed. It is not entirely unlikely that the short history of the responsibility to protect might end at the United Nations without ever being able to demonstrate its potential to settle the debt owed to the peoples of the world by the organization since its foundation.

2. *History of the responsibility to protect*

2.1 Establishment of the United Nations after World War II

Any consideration of the possible role and contribution of the United Nations in preventing and halting genocide, war crimes, ethnic cleansing and crimes against humanity, as stated in the Summit Outcome document, has to take into account the main objectives of the organization, the ideas behind the Charter and their historic context.

The foundation of the United Nations was a response to the common experience of the Second World War and a desire to avert similar horrors in the future. It has been estimated that 55 million people were killed; 35 million wounded and that 3 million went missing during the greatest war in history. 20 to 30 million civilians had been killed, the majority through the Holocaust, forced labor and concentration camps, acts of revenge, deportation and displacement. The allied powers concluded that history has shown too often that political regimes, which act repressively towards their own population tend to follow an aggressive foreign policy in the long term. Lack of development, inflation and unemployment increase the acceptance of discrimination against vulnerable groups and repressive government policies. The Charter reflects awareness of the interrelationship between the respect for human rights and international peace and security. Thus, it contains not only institution-

19 Kofi A. Annan, A Glass At Least Half Full, Wall Street Journal, 19 September 2005.

setting provisions, but establishes fundamental norms for the behavior of States in their international relations. With regard to human rights, the Preamble reaffirms

> faith in fundamental human rights, in the dignity and worth of the human person [and] in the equal rights of men and women.[20]

At the same time, the Charter provides that in their international relations Member States should refrain from the threat or use of force against the territorial integrity or political independence of any state. It allows for only two exceptions, i.e. self-defense and the adoption of legally binding measures by the Security Council, including military measures, in cases of threats to the peace, breaches of the peace, and acts of aggression. However, the latter powers of the Organization are balanced again by the principles of national sovereignty, non-intervention in internal affairs of states and of friendly relations and cooperation among states. The principle of non-intervention is limited to matters essentially within the domestic jurisdiction of States and, thus, its scope of application depends on the development of public international law. Early in the history of the United Nations, the protection from gross and systematic human rights violations, the question of genocide, the right to non-discrimination and the right to self-determination have been considered to lie outside the principle of non-intervention.[21]

During the Cold War the provisions of the Charter were read narrowly. This tendency was supported by the process of decolonization. Many new Member States entered the Organization, conscious of their fragility. Their governments considered the principle of non-intervention a defense against threats and pressures from former colonial powers and their allies.[22]

Notwithstanding this unfavorable environment for joint international action through the United Nations, it was possible to develop a clear body of precedent for peacekeeping which did not fall into either of the categories of exception for military action. Member States widely accepted the use of armed forces under the aegis of the United Nations, if all parties consented to the presence of the mission, the peacekeepers retained impartiality and the use of force was limited to a last resort and only applied in self defense.[23] On this basis, the United Nations have contributed through its operations to bring peace and democracy to countries like Cambodia, El Salvador, Namibia and Mozambique. Peacekeepers also served as a stabilizing factor in conflict areas such as Cyprus, the Golan Heights, Lebanon, Western Sahara and between India and Pakistan.

20 Charter of the United Nations, Preamble, para. 2.

21 *Ian Brownlie*, Principles of Public International Law, Fifth Edition, Oxford University Press, 1998, p. 293 et seq.

22 *Michael Fowler/ Julie Marie Bunck*, Law, Power, and the Sovereign State: The Evolution and Application of the Concept of Sovereignty, Penn State Press, 1995.

23 See for more details *United Nations* (ed.), The Blue Helmets. A Review of United Nations Peace-keeping, Second edition, 1990; *Marrack Goulding*, The Evolution of United Nations Peacekeeping, International Affairs, Vol. 69, 1993, p. 451 et seq.

With the end of the Cold War and the intervention of the international community defending Kuwait against Iraqi occupation, many Member States expected the United Nations finally to establish an international order according to the Charter. Instead, the nature of conflict changed and the problems dominating the 1990s were civil war and massive internal violence. In these new circumstances, the well-established concept of peacekeeping and with it the United Nations as a whole were severely discredited by the 'collective failure' to prevent the killing of thousands of civilians in Rwanda in 1994 and in the Bosnian town of Srebrenica in 1995.[24] Reports commissioned by the Secretariat clearly established that the concept of peacekeeping was not an adequate response to the planned and systematic killing and expulsion of civilians:

> The UN tried to create – or imagine – an environment in which the tenets of peacekeeping – agreement between the parties, deployment by consent and impartiality – could be upheld. [...] An arms embargo with humanitarian aid and the development of a peacekeeping force [...] were poor substitutes for more decisive and forceful action. [...] The cardinal lesson is that a deliberate and systematic attempt to terrorize, expel or murder an entire people must be met decisively with all necessary means.[25]

Since the beginning of the1990s, the Security Council has authorized military action by individual Member States for humanitarian purposes, e.g. in Somalia, Haiti, Rwanda and former Yugoslavia. However, Member States could not agree on a general principle that allowed the use of military force in a country without the consent of the government in order to prevent gross and continuing violations of basic human rights of the country's population.[26] The discussion about such a right dates back to the 19th century or even the Roman Empire.[27]

Since the foundation of the United Nations, Member States have carried out military activities considered under the terms of 'humanitarian intervention', including the intervention of India in East Pakistan, Viet Nam in Cambodia, Tanzania in Uganda and France in Central Africa. In the cases of unilateral action by India and Viet Nam respectively, neither State claimed humanitarian reasons to justify their intervention. Instead, both governments referred to their right to self-defense as an exception established by the Charter itself. However, since the brutality of the Army of West Pakistan as well as the suppression by the Pol Pot regime were well known among Member States, discussions of both situations centered upon the question whether the interventions were justified with a view to the grave and serious violations of human rights and humanitarian law committed by the respective governments against their own population. In the case of Viet Nam in particular, Western countries and Member States of NATO argued that the

24 See Press Release SG/SM/9245, AFR/893, HR/CN/1077.

25 Report of the Secretary-General pursuant to General Assembly resolution 53/35: the fall of Srebrenica, U.N. Doc. A/54/549 of 15 November 1999.

26 *Simon Chesterman*, Just War or Just Peace: Humanitarian intervention and international law, Oxford University Press, 2001.

27 See *Gory J. Bass*, Freedoms Battle: The Origins of Humanitarian Intervention, 2008.

fundamental political consequences of the intervention for the Pol Pot regime were unacceptable, notwithstanding the severe human rights violations.

In the 1990s, the Security Council authorized military action based on resolutions, which established that gross and serious violations of international human rights and humanitarian law could constitute a threat to international peace and security, such as Saddam Hussein's repression of the Kurds and Shia[28], the plight of the Somali people[29], acts of the oppressive regime in Haiti[30] or the ethnic cleansing in Bosnia and Herzegovina[31]. The practice of the Security Council strengthened the view of some Member States that the international community had a right to restrain governments inflicting gross, flagrant and continuing violations of human rights on their own people.

However, the Council could not agree on authorizing NATO action in Kosovo in 1999 notwithstanding its previous affirmation that the deteriorating situation in Kosovo constituted a threat to peace and security in the region[32].

The lack of Security Council action regarding the situation in Kosovo generated a more general debate about the gap between legality and legitimacy, i.e. how to react to gross and systematic violations of human rights, if States continued to claim that humanitarian intervention was violating their sovereignty.[33] Secretary-General Kofi Annan felt strongly that the lack of action in situations of gross violations of human rights could threaten the legitimacy of the United Nations and the authority of the Security Council with its primary responsibility for the maintenance of international peace and security. Following the experience in Kosovo, he summarized his concerns and the challenges for the United Nations as follows:

> 'The inability of the international community in Kosovo to reconcile these two equally compelling interests - universal legitimacy and effectiveness in defense of human rights - has revealed the core challenge to the SC and the UN as a whole in the next century: to forge unity behind the principle that massive and systematic violations of human rights - wherever they may take place - should not be allowed to stand.'[34]

28 S/RES/688 (1991) of 5 April 1991.
29 S/RES/794 (1992) of 3 December 1992.
30 S/RES/940 (1994) of 31 July 1994.
31 S/RES/836 (1993) of 4 June 1993, S/RES/844 (1993) of 18 June 1993. Pakistan and Venezuela requested enforcement of the safe areas by the United Nations. They argued that force authorized under Chapter VII of the Charter had not to be interpreted narrowly and limited to the provision of humanitarian assistance based on the consent even of the perpetrators of aggression, but should include air strikes. See Srebrenica report, FN. 25, paras. 71, 83, 84.
32 S/RES/1198 (1999) of 16 September 1998.
33 *Independent International Commission on Kosovo*, Kosovo Report, Oxford, 2000.
34 Kofi Annan, Two Concepts of Sovereignty, Address to the 54th Session of the General Assembly, reprinted in: *United Nations* (ed.), The Question of Intervention: Statements by the Secretary-General of the United Nations Kofi Annan, New York, 1999, p. 39 et seq.

2.2 The International Commission on Intervention and State Sovereignty (ICISS)

In response to this dilemma, the Canadian government sponsored the International Commission on Intervention and State Sovereignty (ICISS) which presented its report, entitled 'The Responsibility to Protect', to the Secretary-General at the end of 2001. The final Report of the Commission summarized twelve months of intensive research and deliberations in a concise document encapsulating the Commissioners' views on intervention and state sovereignty and their recommendations for practical action.[35]

The Commission was established as an independent international body and mandated to help bridging the concepts of intervention and state sovereignty through a broader understanding of the relevant issues and to foster a global political consensus towards action within the UN system. The Commission convened five full meetings and, in order to stimulate debate and ensure that the Commission heard the broadest possible range of views during the course of its work, eleven roundtables and national consultations were held in all regions of the world. An advisory board of serving and former foreign ministers and other dignitaries, chaired by former Canadian Foreign Minister Lloyd Axworthy was appointed to serve as the political reference point for Commissioners and to provide the ICISS with overall political guidance during its mandate.[36]

In summary, the report of the Commission made several important contributions to the international policy debate on human rights versus sovereignty. Most importantly, it turned the debate about a 'right to intervene' into a 'responsibility to protect' people at grave risk. This change of perspective intended to move the attention away from the interveners and to the potential victims needing support. Sovereignty, the Committee argued, involved not just 'control' but 'responsibility'. Building on important contributions made by Bernard Kouchner, Francis Deng and others during the 1990s, the Commission established that the State itself had the primary responsibility to protect the individuals within it; but where it failed, through either lack of capacity or will, that responsibility to protect shifted to the wider international community.[37] Furthermore, the ICISS defined the responsibility to protect as a continuum of measures constituted by the responsibility to prevent, the responsibility to react and the responsibility to rebuild. This continuum of measures should prevent short-term military intervention based on short-term political interests and move the discussion away from concentrating on such

35 *ICISS*, The Responsibility to Protect, Ottawa, 2002.

36 Details of the methodology and the procedure of the Commission are summarized in: *ICISS*, The Responsibility to Protect. Research, Bibliography, Background, Ottawa, 2002, p. 339 et seq.

37 See *Mario Bettati/ Bernard Kouchner* (eds.), Le devoir d'ingerence, Paris, 1987, p. 300; *Francis M. Deng/ Sadikiel Kimaro/ Terrence Lyons/ Donald Rothchild/ I. William* (eds.), Sovereignty as Responsibility: Conflict Management in Africa, Washington, 1996.

scenarios. Finally, the Commission proposed a set of criteria for any decision on military intervention.[38]

The Commission's report found a positive resonance among international commentators, lawyers and Non-Governmental Organizations (NGOs). In the assessment of Gareth Evans, the Co-Chair of the Commission, the report, which was published in December 2001, was 'almost suffocated' in the immediate aftermath of the events in the United States on 11 September 2001 and the massive international preoccupation with terrorism rather than internal mass atrocities.[39]

2.3 The High-level Panel on Threats, Challenges and Change

Secretary-General Kofi Annan announced the establishment of the Panel on Threats, Challenges and Change in a letter, dating 3 November 2003, addressed to the President of the General Assembly. He indicated that the Panel was

> tasked with examining the major threats and challenges the world faces in the broad field of peace and security, including economic and social issues insofar as they relate to peace and security, and making recommendations for the elements of a collective response.

The aim of the Panel was to recommend practical measures for effective collective action, based upon an analysis of future threats to peace and security, an appraisal of the contribution that collective action could make and a thorough assessment of existing approaches, instruments and mechanisms. The Panel was not asked to formulate policies on specific issues, nor on the role of the United Nations in specific places. Rather, it was expected to provide a new assessment of the challenges ahead and to recommend the changes required to meet them through collective action. The Panel held six meetings in addition to a number of regional consultations and workshops throughout the world. The final report was presented to the Secretary-General on 1 December 2004 and to the General Assembly the next day.[40]

The Panel referred to the responsibility to protect in the context of the legality of the involvement of the United Nations in cases of internal threats. It

> endorse[d] the emerging norm that there is a collective international responsibility to protect, exercisable by the Security Council authorizing military intervention as a last resort, in the event of genocide and other large scale killing, ethnic cleansing or serious violations of

38 See for an assessment of the ICISS concept e.g. *Amitav Acharya*, Redefining the Dilemmas of Humanitarian Intervention, Australian Journal of International Affairs, No.56, 2002, p.373 et seq.

39 Gareth Evans, From Humanitarian Intervention to the Responsibility to Protect. Keynote Address on Symposium on Humanitarian Intervention, University of Wisconsin, Madison, 31 March 2006, available at http://www.crisisgroup.org/home/index.cfm?id=4521&l=1.

40 A more secure world: our shared responsibility. Report of the High-level Panel on Threats, Challenges and Change, U.N.-Doc. A/59/565 of 17 November 2004.

> international humanitarian law which sovereign Governments have proven powerless or unwilling to prevent.[41]

According to the Panel, the primary focus should be on assisting the cessation of violence through mediation and the protection of people through measures such as humanitarian, human rights and police missions. Force should be used only as a last resort. In the context of the question of legitimacy, the Panel recommended that the Security Council should adopt a set of guidelines, similar to those proposed by the ICISS, for decisions on the use of force. The Panel argued that such guidelines could contribute to achieving consensus on the use of coercive action, including armed force, maximize international support for Security Council decisions and minimize unilateral action of Member States.[42] The Panel asked the permanent members of the Security Council to refrain from the use of the veto in cases of genocide and large-scale human rights abuses.[43]

2.4 In Larger Freedom

In March 2005, the Secretary-General submitted to Member States a report on the implementation of the Millennium Declaration in preparation for the Summit in September.[44] The report referred to the responsibility to protect in the context of the promotion of the rule of law, human rights and democracy and urged Member States to embrace and act on the responsibility to protect potential or actual victims of massive atrocities.[45] The Secretary-General refrained from further qualifying the responsibility to protect as either an emerging norm or a concept. While he referred to the High-level Panel report in this context, the Secretary-General did not consider the responsibility to protect in the context of peace and security or the responsibilities of the Security Council. He did neither suggest the adoption of criteria for a decision on the use of force nor appealed for restrictions on the use of the veto. At the same time, the Secretary-General acknowledged the 'sensitivities involved in this issue'.[46]

2.5 Conclusions

The history of the responsibility to protect in the United Nations has been very successful with regard to the little time that passed between the publication of the

41 High-level Panel report, op. cit., para. 203.
42 Op. cit., para. 206.
43 Op. cit., para. 256.
44 In Larger Freedom: towards development, security and human rights for all. Report of the Secretary-General, U.N.-Doc. A/59/2005 of 25 March 2005.
45 Op. cit., para. 132.
46 Op. cit., para. 135.

ICISS report and the inclusion of respective wording in the Summit Outcome document. However, this fast turn-over might have been caused by dropping important elements of the original concept on the way to a consensus document. The Secretary-General was keen on preserving the concept for inclusion in the Summit Document and, thus, chose a presentation in a context that was acceptable for all Member States. While some details of its exact content and implementation could be left to a later stage, other elements altered during the drafting process might turn out to be essential for future implementation.

In order to assess the opportunities of the agreement on the responsibility to protect in the Summit Outcome document, there is a need to review the status of existing legal obligations to protect populations from genocide, war crimes and crimes against humanity.

3. The responsibility to protect deconstructed – concept and legal content

There is broad agreement that the responsibility to protect builds on existing legal obligations related to genocide, war crimes, ethnic cleansing and crimes against humanity.[47] With a view to the limited sources of international law, the question of the possible form and content of an additional norm on the responsibility to protect must be raised, including the nature of obligations it could entail for Member States and the United Nations. Finally, the added value of the responsibility to protect has to be considered carefully in the light of the experience of past failures of the United Nations in preventing or halting genocide, war crimes, ethnic cleansing and crimes against humanity.

3.1 The three 'dimensions' to prevent, react and rebuild

It has been considered a main achievement of the responsibility to protect as presented in the ICISS report to have extended the focus of attention beyond military intervention to a continuum of steps, including the responsibility to prevent (to address both the root causes and direct causes of internal conflicts and other man-made crises); the responsibility to react (to respond to situations of compelling human need with appropriate measures, which may include coercive measures like sanctions and international prosecution, and in extreme cases military intervention); and the responsibility to rebuild (to provide, particularly after a military intervention, full assistance for recovery, reconstruction and reconciliation).

These three dimensions of the responsibility to protect have not been reflected in the wording of the Summit Outcome document and Secretary-General Ban Ki-moon

47 See on the key elements of the responsibility to protect e.g. *Sabine von Schorlemer*, The Responsibility to Protect as an Element of Peace. Recommendations for its Operationalization, Development and Peace Foundation, Policy Paper 28, 2007, p. 5 et seq.

interpreted the agreement to rest on 'three pillars' not identical with the ICISS concept.[48] However, the three dimensions have been very prominent in discussions on the operationalization of the responsibility to protect among Member States and there seems to be agreement that they represent constituent elements of the agreement.

Thus, any analysis of the possible legal content of the responsibility to protect should consider all three dimensions in order to arrive at a list of obligations that could be recommended and implemented at different stages of a developing crisis. In addition to the specific standards applicable to genocide, war crimes, ethnic cleansing and crimes against humanity, human rights obligations contained in treaties and customary law could be directly relevant for the application of the responsibility to protect. In this regard, there is a need to agree on the time-frame available for preventive action within the responsibility to prevent. One could argue that any activity to prevent human rights violations of specific ethnic, racial, religious or national group would, ultimately, also prevent genocide. The Holocaust was preceded by the implementation of an increasingly repressive system of discrimination against the Jewish population, including the boycott of their businesses and legislation excluding them from certain professions, access to universities and social services.[49] The Committee on the Elimination of Racial Discrimination (CERD) agreed on indicators to detect and prevent developments in racial discrimination that could lead to violent conflict and genocide.[50] While the relevance of long-term human rights and institution building for the prevention of the listed crimes is obvious, the challenge for the United Nations will be the concentration of measure short of military intervention that could be proposed to Member States to prevent immediate or ongoing violence in the short-term. The most relevant rights should be extracted carefully from previous work related to human rights in conflict.[51]

There is a problematic attempt of supporters of the concept by trying to expand its application to other areas of human suffering, including climate change, HIV/ AIDS or general considerations of human security. However, as much as one would wish to find a coherent solution for the lack of implementation of international obligations regarding any life-threatening risk of large numbers of people, the responsibility to protect must not be applied to situations beyond the very narrow scope it was

48 See Report of the Secretary-General on the work of the organization, U.N.-Doc. A/63/1 of 12 August 2008, para. 74 and C.4, below.

49 *Roland Staudinger*, Rassenrecht und Rassenstaat: Die nationalsozialistische Version eines "biologischen totalen Staates", 1999.

50 Declaration on the prevention of genocide, CERD/C/66/1 of 17 October 2005; Decision on follow-up to the Declaration on the prevention of genocide, CERD/C/67/1 of 14 October 2005.

51 See for economic, social and cultural rights e.g. Implementation of General Assembly Resolution 60/251 of 15 March 3006 entitled "Human Rights Council", Question of the realization in all countries of economic, social and cultural rights, Report of the Secretary-General, U.N.-Doc. A/HRC/4/62 of 13 February 2007, para. 27 et seq.

developed for, i.e. exceptional situations similar to Rwanda or Srebrenica. However, the responsibility to prevent should be distinguished from the obligation to prevent human rights violations and defined within its specific and narrow scope. Thus, the review of existing obligations should be limited to the imminent causes of large-scale violence.

At the same time, the three dimensions would constitute a risk for the further development of the responsibility to protect if discussions shifted away from the core question related to military action in order to protect civilian populations from imminent or ongoing violence similar to the events in Rwanda or Srebrenica. After the Summit, many supporters put the responsibility to prevent and the responsibility to rebuild into the center of attention claiming that they formed the core of the concept.[52] Advocates of the responsibility to protect repeated at these occasions that it was 'not about military intervention'. The ICISS is quite clear in this regard, stating that the

> report is about the so-called right to humanitarian intervention: the question of when, if ever, it is appropriate for states to take coercive – and in particular military – action, against another State for the purpose of protecting people at risk in that other State.[53]

When defining the responsibility to prevent, the ICISS distinguished the prevention of root causes for conflict and direct prevention efforts. While the Commission acknowledged the general need for improved prevention capacities within the United Nations, it considered the support of local prevention with a view to creating the necessary credibility for international action beyond prevention, especially when that reaction involved coercive measures and, ultimately, the use of armed force.[54] When dealing with the root cause and direct prevention efforts, the ICISS mainly referred to general considerations on conflict prevention and did not offer particular recommendations.[55]

Following these considerations, the responsibility to protect from the root causes of the listed crimes is an ongoing activity of different United Nations entities within the implementation of their existing mandates. The work of the United Nations Development Programme (UNDP), the United Nations Children's Fund (UNICEF), OHCHR and other departments and agencies towards the establishment of effective rule of law institutions, the training of armed forces, police and other state agents in human rights law, and technical assistance in drafting legislation ultimately contribute as well to the prevention of the listed crimes. It is difficult to imagine how and why their being part of the responsibility to protect could make them more effective. More to the contrary – while governments might be receptive to the benefits of implementing their general human rights obligations, they might be reluctant to accept a need to prevent genocide, war crimes, ethnic cleansing and

52 See e.g. *Gareth Evans*, The Responsibility to Protect. Ending Mass Atrocity Crimes Once and For All, Brookings Institution Press, 2008, p. 56.

53 See http://www.iciss-ciise.gc.ca/report-en.asp

54 ICISS Report, FN. 35, para. 3.4

55 Op. cit., para. 3.18 et seq.

crimes against humanity from taking place in their respective countries in the future. Furthermore, as all activities of the United Nations are based on the interrelated purposes and principles of the Charter,[56] including the prevention of conflict, the responsibility to protect should not replace the broad approach of the Charter by its own limited scope of application.

However, the application of the responsibility to protect on country situations is severely limited by the lack of criteria to identify the risk of massive human rights violations in the medium or longer term.[57]

3.2 Legal content

3.2.1 The responsibility to protect populations from genocide

Genocide is defined in article 1 of the Convention on the Prevention and Punishment of the Crime of Genocide[58] and, more recently, in article 6 of the Rome Statute of the Establishment of an International Criminal Court[59].

In 1933, Raphael Lemkin, a young Polish lawyer, had presented a paper at an international criminal law conference that drew attention to the political rise of Hitler in Germany and the massacre of the Armenian population of the Ottoman Empire. He proposed making the extermination of national, ethnic or religious groups an international crime similar to slavery or piracy.[60] The Nuremberg Tribunal considered the Holocaust as an accessory of the conspiracy to wage aggressive war on a global scale rather than a distinct crime committed by individual perpetrators.[61] Only in 1948, after millions had been slaughtered under circumstances described by Lemkin, the United Nations passed the Convention on the Prevention and Punishment of the Crime of Genocide.[62]

The particular importance of the Convention for possible United Nations action in situations of massive and serious violations of human rights or humanitarian law

56 See article 1 of the United Nations Charter. For details see *Franz Cede/ Lilly Sucharipa-Behrmann* (eds.), The United Nations: Law and Practice, Martinus Nijhoff, 2001, p. 11 et seq.

57 *Evans*, FN. 52 p. 72 et seq. identifies the challenges without offering criteria.

58 Convention on the Prevention and Punishment of the Crime of Genocide, General Assembly resolution 260 A (III) of 9 December 1948.

59 Adopted by the United Nations Diplomatic Conference of Plenipotentiaries on the Establishment of an International Criminal Court on 17 July 1998.

60 Further developed in *Raphael Lemkin*, Genocide, American Scholar, Volume 15, no. 2 (April 1946), p. 227 et seq.

61 See International Military Tribunal, Indictment, Anklagepunkt Drei, Kriegsverbrechen, VIII, Nuremberg, 1946.

62 See for details on the history of the Convention and Lemkin's contribution *Samantha Power*, A Problem from Hell. America and the age of genocide, London, 2002, p. 47 et seq.

derives from the Advisory Opinion of the International Criminal Court on Reservations to the Convention on the Prevention and Punishment of the Crime of Genocide of 1951 in which the Court held that the provisions of the Convention express pre-existing customary international law and obligations erga omnes.[63]

The International Court of Justice drew an essential distinction between the obligations of a State towards the international community as a whole and those arising vis-à-vis another State. The Court clarified that by their very nature the former were the concern of all States and, in view of the importance of the rights involved, all States could claim a legal interest in their protection. Such obligations derived from the outlawing of genocide and from the principles and rules concerning the basic rights of the human person, including the protection from racial discrimination. Some of the corresponding rights of protection had entered into general international law, others derived from international instruments of a universal character.[64]

Furthermore, the Court held that the norm prohibiting genocide constitutes ius cogens and, thus, was binding upon all States regardless of their ratification of signature of the Convention[65].

The Convention focuses more on punishment than on prevention although the former is meant to create a general deterrent through the application of criminal law. In addition, some of the acts referred to in article 3 of the Convention have a preventive dimension, such as the prosecution of conspiracy or attempts of public incitement to commit genocide.

The assessment of the preventive effect of the work of international courts concerning ongoing events on the ground has been mixed. While some claim a general preventive effect of the ad-hoc Tribunals on potential perpetrators, others argue that ethnic cleansing increased in Bosnia and Herzegovina after the International Criminal Tribunal for the former Yugoslavia (ICTY) was created in 1993.[66] After the request by the Prosecutor of the International Criminal Court of an arrest warrant against President Bashir of Sudan, the United Nations noted an increase in cooperation of the Government in Khartoum on technical issues, including visa and customs.[67] However, closer analysis of the possible motives arrived at different causes, some entirely unrelated to the Court procedure. Overall, empirical data will be difficult to extract, as political decision making is determined

63 Advisory Opinion on Reservations to the Genocide Convention, ICJ Reports 1951, p. 23 et seq.

64 Barcelona Traction, Light and Power Company, Limited (Belgium vs. Spain), judgment of 5 February 1970, ICJ Reports 1970, p. 3, para. 33 et seq.

65 The Court confirmed its earlier statements of 1951 and 1996 in the judgment of 6 February 2006 in the case of Armed Activities on the Territory of the Congo (New Application 2002) (Democratic Republic of the Congo vs. Rwanda), General List No. 126, para. 64.

66 *Payam Akhavan*, Beyond Impunity: Can International Criminal Justice Prevent Future Atrocities?, AJIL Vol. 95, 2001, p. 7 et seq.

67 See International Criminal Court, Pre-Trial Chamber I, Situation in Darfur, The Sudan, Public Redacted Version of the Prosecutor's Application under Article 58, ICC-02/05 of 14 July 2008.

by facts as much as perceptions or expectations. The responsibility to protect could provide the framework for preventing and halting crimes that fall under the jurisdiction of the International Criminal Court.

Another preventive element can be found in article 8, which provides for the possibility of any contracting party to call upon the competent organs of the United Nations to take action on the prevention or repression of acts of genocide. The International Court of Justice found that governments are obliged to take all measures within their power to prevent the commission of the crime of genocide, even before a competent court determines that the Convention actually applies to a case at hand.[68]

In the absence of any particular guidance on the content of the obligation to prevent genocide, the relevant organs of the United Nations never applied the Convention. There was a historic opportunity, when Secretary-General Kofi Annan argued in the 5040th meeting of the Security Council on Darfur that, for the first time, the Council had been seized under article 8 of the Convention,[69] but the Members of the Council did not follow this line of reasoning. Furthermore, Member States lacked interest in creating a special body supervising the implementation of the Convention similar to the treaty bodies provided for in the different human rights treaties.[70]

In its judgment in the case of Bosnia and Herzegovina v. Serbia and Montenegro the International Court of Justice finally identified specific obligations of States to prevent and punish genocide.[71] The Court held that while one of the most effective ways to prevent criminal behavior was to criminalize and punish it effectively, the obligation to prevent genocide was of a free standing nature. The obligation had a scope beyond the duty to punish and beyond the right to call on the competent organs of the United Nations to take appropriate action.

Based on the principles that emerge from the judgment, some concrete obligations of Member States to prevent and punish genocide can be established. The International Court of Justice did not determine whether the specific preventive obligations set out in its judgment apply also as a matter of customary international law. However, as the general obligations set out in the Convention reflect customary law, their concretization should not be limited to the application of the Convention either.

68 Case Concerning the Application of the Convention on the Prevention and Punishment of the Crime of Genocide (Bosnia and Herzegovina v. Yugoslavia (Serbia and Montenegro)) (Request for the indication of provisional measures), ICJ Reports 1993, p. 52, para. 46.

69 Press Release SC/8191.

70 See most recently Views of States parties to the Convention on the Prevention and Punishment of the Crime of Genocide on the Secretary-General's proposal that they consider setting up a committee on the prevention of genocide, Note by the Secretariat, U.N.-Doc. E/CN.4/2005/46 of 10 December 2004.

71 Case Concerning the Application of the Convention on the Prevention and Punishment of the Crime of Genocide (Bosnia and Herzegovina v. Serbia and Montenegro), Judgment of 26 February 2007, General List No. 91.

In general, the Court found that it is not an absolute obligation to succeed in preventing genocide. The State must take all measures that are within its power and which might contribute to preventing genocide. For the obligation to prevent genocide to be triggered the State does not have to be certain that genocide is occurring or is about to be committed. It is sufficient that the State is aware, or should be aware, of a serious danger.[72]

As priority, the State must ensure that its own organs and officials as well as individuals or groups under its control do not commit genocide. In relation to others not under its direction, the State must use all reasonable means available to prevent genocide as far as possible. However, the obligation to prevent includes more indirect causes as States must not e.g. supply weapons to another State knowing that they will be used in committing genocide. The obligation to prevent is defined by the capacity of the State to influence the persons committing, or likely to commit, genocide. While the State's capacity will normally be greater within its own territory, it can be engaged in respect to events outside its borders based on geographical proximity and the strength of political or military links.[73]

Should prevention fail, States must prosecute and punish perpetrators of the crime of genocide, pursuant to Article 1 of the Convention. To this end, States must establish jurisdiction over all acts of genocide occurring in their territory. With a view to the preventive function of criminal law, States must provide for effective penalties for those found guilty.

Where a specialized tribunal such as the International Criminal Tribunal for Rwanda (ICTR) or ICTY is mandated to prosecute and punish individuals allegedly responsible for the commission of the crime of genocide, States have an obligation to cooperate with that tribunal, including to arrest and transfer indictees within their jurisdiction. The International Court of Justice determined that Serbia had violated its obligation to ensure punishment under the Convention through failing to arrest and transfer Mladić and Karadžić to the ICTY. States Parties to the Rome Statute had an obligation to cooperate with the International Criminal Court, including on the arrest and transfer of indictees within their jurisdiction. This obligation extends to situations referred to the International Criminal Court by the Security Council under Chapter VII of the Charter.[74]

Additional specific obligations deriving from the general obligation to prevent and punish genocide could be identified through a systematic review of decisions of the ICTY and ICTR. Prevention of genocide may as well entail other rights and obligations that are only implicit in the Convention. General human rights

72 Case Concerning the Application of the Convention on the Prevention and Punishment of the Crime of Genocide (Bosnia and Herzegovina v. Serbia and Montenegro), Judgment of 26 February 2007, para. 425 et seq.

73 Op. cit., para. 166 et seq.,

74 See article 13 (b) of the Rome Statute. On 31 March 2005, the Security Council referred the situation in Darfur since 1 July 2002 to the Prosecutor of the International Criminal Court. The text of the resolution, U.N.-Doc. S/RES/1593 (2005), quoted article 16 instead of article 13 (b) in order to allow the United States to let the referral pass.

instruments related to hate propaganda, disbanding of racist organizations or preparatory acts required to commit genocide could establish important duties in the circumstances of a particular country situation.[75]

3.2.2 The responsibility to protect populations from war crimes

Usually, the term war crimes refers to grave breaches of the four Geneva Conventions and other serious violations of the laws and customs applicable in armed conflict. A more recent definition of war crimes can be found in article 8 of the Rome Statute.

The International Court of Justice identified an extensive body of customary international law applicable in international armed conflicts,[76] codified in the Hague Regulations and the four Geneva Conventions, and the main provisions of the Additional Protocol I to the Conventions.[77]

While the extent of customary international law applicable in non-international armed conflicts is less certain, a minimum includes the provisions of common Article 3 to the four Geneva Conventions – the obligation to treat humanely all persons taking no active part in hostilities. Further provisions derive from the Additional Protocol II to the Conventions. According to the Study on Customary International Humanitarian Law by the International Committee of the Red Cross, many of the customary rules applicable in international armed conflict, meanwhile, are also applicable in non-international armed conflicts.[78]

A catalogue of recognized war crimes reflects the horrors that armed conflict causes to soldiers, uninvolved civilians, livelihoods, infrastructure and cultural heritage.[79] On the one hand they include serious violations of human rights and humanitarian law such as willful killing, torture or inhuman treatment, rape, forced prostitution or forced pregnancy, subjecting detainees to mutilation, or medical or scientific experiments and enlisting and using child soldiers. On the other hand, some crimes merely refer to violations of the conduct of war or the proportionality of means employed for military purposes, such as launching attacks which cause excessive loss of life or injury in relation to the anticipated military advantage, employing weapons, projectiles and material and methods of warfare which are of a nature to cause superfluous injury or unnecessary suffering.

75 See for details *William A. Schabas*, Genocide in International Law (2000), p. 447 et seq.

76 Advisory Opinion on the legality of the Threat or Use of Nuclear Weapons, ICJ Reports (1996) 226, at p. 257.

77 Protocol Additional to the Geneva Conventions of 12 August 1949, and Relating to the protection of Victims of Non-International Armed Conflicts.

78 *Jean-Marie Henckaerts/ Louise Doswald-Beck*, Customary International Humanitarian Law, Cambridge, 2005, pp. 457- 475. See for details *Larry Maybee/ Benarji Chakka*, Custom as Source of International Humanitarian Law, ICRC New Delhi, 2006.

79 *Roy Gutman/ David Rief* (eds.), Crimes of War. What the Public Should Know, New York, 1999.

With a view to the particular application envisioned for the responsibility to protect, it would be important to identify those war crimes falling out of the scope of relevant obligations.

The primary source of States' obligations to prevent war crimes is common article 1 of the Geneva Conventions stipulating the obligation 'to respect' and 'ensure respect' for the Conventions 'in all circumstances'. The same provision is reiterated in article 1 of Additional Protocol I. The International Court of Justice held that common article 1 reflects customary international law and a general principle of humanitarian law applicable also in non-international armed conflicts.[80] According to the ICTY, the provision establishes erga omnes obligation for States.[81] It has also been regarded an obligation for all States, whether or not parties to a conflict, to take all possible steps to ensure that the rules of humanitarian law are respected by all.[82]

Similar to the specific obligations to protect and punish genocide, specific obligations can be deducted from the general obligation to respect and ensure respect for the Geneva Conventions.

States must ensure that their organs and officials, in particular their armed forces do not commit war crimes, whether within the national territory or beyond. To this end, States must make available legal advisers to military commanders on the application of international humanitarian law. Military commanders must be required to prevent the commission of war crimes by forces under their command and other persons under their control, and to report any breaches. In addition to their responsibility for regular armed forces, States must neither direct nor exercise control over individuals and groups, within or beyond the national territory, to commit war crimes. As in the case of genocide, 'control' refers to overall control of a general character, not specific control over particular acts.[83] Beyond its own involvement in armed conflict, States must not encourage the commission of war crimes by parties to armed conflict, and must exert their influence to prevent or halt any such violations.[84]

With regard to the prosecution and punishment of war crimes States must enact legislation to implement their international humanitarian law obligations, including for the prosecution and effective punishment of those committing war crimes or ordering them to be committed, and disseminate it in peacetime and time of armed conflict, both to the armed forces and to the civilian population. States must investigate any alleged war crime allegedly committed by their nationals, by their armed forces, or on their territory and prosecute the suspects.[85] In addition, States must search for persons alleged to have committed war crimes, of whatever

80 Military and Paramilitary Activities in and against Nicaragua, ICJ Reports 1986, para. 220

81 See e.g. the ICTY judgment in Kupreskić, 14 January 2000, case No. IT-95-16-T paras 517 and 519; ICRC Customary Law Study, FN. 78, rule 140.

82 This view is not universally shared by States.

83 ICTY, Tadić, Judgment of 15 July 1999, Case No. IT-94-1, paras 109 and 115-116.

84 ICRC Customary Law Study, FN. 78, rule 144.

85 Op. cit., rules 157 and 158.

nationality, and where appropriate bring them before their national courts.[86] States must cooperate with each other, to the extent possible, to facilitate the investigation of war crimes and the prosecution of the suspects.[87] If the State does not prosecute before its own courts, it shall extradite the suspects to another State where a prima facie case has been established.[88] Statutes of limitation do not apply to war crimes.[89]

The obligations regarding the cooperation with special tribunals and the International Criminal Court are the same as those for genocide.

3.2.3 The responsibility to protect populations from crimes against humanity

While some references to crimes against humanity date back several centuries, the term was used in a context relevant for the responsibility to protect by the Allied powers when denouncing the massacre of the Armenian population in 1915. The term reappeared in the Nuremberg Charter in 1945.[90] Today, crimes against humanity are deemed to be part of international ius cogens and, thus, constitute non-derogable rules of international law. So far, States did not draft a specialized international convention as a source for obligations to prevent and punish crimes against humanity. However, this category of crimes has been included in the statutes of the ICTY, the ICTR and the Special Court for Sierra Leone (SCSL)[91] and their status has been considered extensively by these courts. The most recent definition of crimes against humanity can be found in article 7 of the Rome Statute. According to their origin as the most serious crimes of concern to the whole world, crimes against humanity include the widespread or systematic extermination, enslavement, deportation, torture, rape, forced prostitution or persecution of civilians.[92] More precise obligations derive from the case law of the tribunals.

Similar to the obligations related to the protection from genocide and war crimes, States must ensure that their organs and officials do not commit crimes against humanity. To this end, States must not condone or tolerate any policy of widespread or systematic attacks against the civilian population by their organs or officials and prevent the commission of crimes against humanity by others within their jurisdiction. Beyond their organs and officials, States must not instruct, direct nor exercise overall control over groups or individuals to commit crimes against

86 E.g. article 146 Geneva Convention IV.

87 Op. cit., rule 161.

88 E.g. article 146 Geneva Convention IV.

89 Op. cit., rule 160.

90 Benjamin Ferencz, From Nuremberg to Rome: A Personal Account, in: *Mark Lattimer/ Philippe Sands* (eds.), Justice for Crimes against Humanity, Oxford, 2003, p. 31 et seq.

91 See article 2 of the Statute of the Special Court for Sierra Leone, Report of the Secretary-General on the establishment of a Special Court for Sierra Leone, Enclosure, U.N.-Doc. S/2000/914 of 4 October 2000, p. 21 et seq.

92 *William A. Schabas*, An Introduction to the International Criminal Court, Second Edition, Cambridge University Press, 2004, p. 41 et seq.

humanity. In addition, States must not aid or assist other States to commit crimes against humanity, e.g. through supplying weapons in the knowledge that they are being used for this purpose.

It is noteworthy that these obligations lack some of the progressive aspects identified by the International Court of Justice in relation to States' obligations to prevent the crime of genocide. In relation to the crime of genocide, the obligation to use influence over individuals or groups extends beyond national territory, arises before it is certain that genocide is being committed and includes all actions that might help prevent genocide from being committed.

According to the case law of the ad-hoc tribunals further obligations imposed on States are more limited than those with respect to the crime of genocide and entail primarily that States must provide for the prosecution and punishment of those committing crimes against humanity. To this end, they must take jurisdiction over crimes against humanity occurring on their territory, but are not obliged to establish universal jurisdiction.[93]

As with the crime of genocide and war crimes, States have an obligation of cooperation where an international court or tribunal has jurisdiction, including an obligation to arrest and transfer indictees within their jurisdiction.

3.2.4 The responsibility to protect populations from ethnic cleansing

The term 'ethnic cleansing' has been employed to refer to the events in Bosnia and Herzegovina at the beginning of the 1990s[94] and has been used in UN practice as

> rendering an area ethnically homogeneous by using force or intimidation to remove persons of given groups from the area.[95]

When columns of civilians with their belongings loaded on nearly-collapsing vehicles or donkeys streamed out of destroyed villages in Kosovo or Darfur, civil society and media referred to ethnic cleansing to draw attention to the gravity of the situation.

The term ethnic cleansing has no immediate legal significance. However, different practices constituting the act of ethnic cleansing, such as the destruction of houses, crops or wells, widespread sexual violence or killings, can be qualified as grave breaches of the Geneva Conventions, war crimes, crimes against humanity and, in certain circumstances, even genocide. The breaches of international humanitarian law closely aligned to the practice of ethnic cleansing are deportation and forcible transfer. Ethnic cleansing may also be achieved by carrying out a

93 ICTY, Furundzija, Judgment of 10 December 1998, Case No. IT-95-17/1-T, para 142.

94 See U.N.-Doc. S/RES/787 (1992) of 16 November 1992, para. 2; S/RES/827 (1993) of 25 May 1993, preamble; A/RES/47/121 of 18 December 1992.

95 Interim report of the Commission of Experts Established Pursuant to Security Council Resolution 780 (1992), U.N.-Doc. S/35374 (1993), para. 55.

violent campaign, which has the effect of forcing the population to flee a certain territory.

Acts of deportation or forcible transfer are prohibited according to article 48 of the Geneva Convention IV and are considered grave breaches under article 147. Pursuant to Article 146, States have an obligation to prevent grave breaches of the Geneva Conventions by way of passing and enacting any legislation necessary to provide effective penal sanctions to persons committing or ordering any of these acts. States have a duty to search for persons alleged to have committed, or to have ordered to be committed, such grave breaches. Finally, they have the obligation to bring responsible persons before their own courts, regardless of their nationality or to extradite such persons for trial to another High Contracting Party.

State parties to the Geneva Conventions and the Additional Protocols are bound by their provisions as a matter of conventional law, but it is only grave breaches that give rise to an obligation for States to criminalize, prosecute or extradite. The other acts prohibited do not give rise to individual criminal responsibility under the relevant treaties, but may do so under customary international law. [96]

Thus, the responsibility to protect populations from ethnic cleansing is already part of the responsibility to protect populations from genocide, war crimes and crimes against humanity. Therefore, in the following it will no longer be listed as a separate crime. Hopefully, the identification of ethnic cleansing as a separate case for the application of the responsibility to protect will enable the international community to address some situations based on their factual appearance rather than their legal qualifications.

3.3 The possible form and content of a norm on responsibility to protect

With a view to the High-level Panel Report, the responsibility to protect is often referred to as an 'emerging norm of international law'. Notwithstanding the rejection of this wording during the negotiations of the Summit Outcome, the legal effect of the provision in the Summit Outcome on the responsibility to protect remains an important part of the discussion on its operationalization by the United Nations.

According to article 38 of the Statute of the International Court of Justice, the sources of international law are limited to international treaties, custom and general principles of law. Customary international law requires a general practice of States accompanied by opinio juris.

The Summit Outcome was adopted by the General Assembly by resolution, which is a non-binding recommendation for Member States. In some instances, resolutions of the General Assembly constitute evidence of customary international law or contribute to its formation. However, resolutions of the General Assembly do not create new rules of customary international law as such. In addition, they can

96 See e.g. ICTY, Krnojelac, Appeal Judgment, Case no. IT-97-25-A, para. 220.

make an important contribution to the development of international treaties by developing main principles for future agreements. Thus resolutions of the General Assembly often function as a starting point, frame or concept for discussions establishing or creating international law.[97]

Some consider the creation of customary international law, if States confirmed their perceived legal conviction through actual behavior outside the organization. Others claim that the necessary state practice as evidence for the existence for customary international law would be manifest already, when the State voted for the resolution in question. Even though the formation of human rights or humanitarian obligations through customary law will always be challenged by the violation of the rule in question, at least, state practice should evidence general recognition of a legal obligation.[98] According to the International Court of Justice, resolutions can provide evidence for the existence of a certain rule or of emergence of opinio juris.[99]

In very rare cases, States might have had the clear intention to lay down a legal provision in a resolution of the General Assembly. However, those exceptional circumstances could only be considered if those States with particular interests in the issue agreed to the rule in question.[100] Clearly, the negotiations on the Summit Outcome did not provide evidence to claim such exceptional circumstances.

Regarding the possible content of a legal provision on the responsibility to protect in the Summit Outcome, in general, international norms set out certain principles and obligations for States to act or omit certain action. With regard to genocide, war crimes, ethnic cleansing and crimes against humanity, the obligations to omit and act are contained already in the respective legal standards many of which attained the character of peremptory norms of international law.

Many point at an additional obligation of the international community created by the Summit Outcome to protect civilian populations from those crimes. This is considered a new international norm separate from existing legal obligations.[101] According to this line of argument, the responsibility to protect discarded the notion of a right to intervene by configuring a permanent duty to protect individuals against abusive behavior. The onus of protection fell by default on the international community and encompassed a continuum of prevention, reaction and commitment to rebuild. This norm was engaged from the earliest stages of a situation of concern. The most serious implication of this norm was that all States were now burdened with the responsibility to take action and could no longer claim a discretionary right

97 On the legal nature and legal effect of resolutions of the General Assembly see Hailbronner/ Klein, Art. 10 in: *Bruno Simma*, The Charter of the United Nations, 2nd ed., Oxford University Press, 2002, para. 43 et seq.

98 North Sea Continental Shelf, ICJ Reports 1969, p. 43.

99 Legality of the Threat or Use of Nuclear Weapons, Advisory Opinion, ICJ Reports 1996, p. 254.

100 Hailbronner/ Klein, op. cit., para. 57.

101 See on the following in particular Louise Arbour, The Responsibility to Protect as a duty of care in international law and practice, Trinity College Dublin, 23 November 2007.

to intervene. Ultimately, this responsibility rested upon the obligation to prevent and punish genocide.

The United Nations Charter provides for the requirements and limits of collective action against a Member State in article 39 and 40. The practice of the Security Council on these provisions has led to the controversial discussion about the lawfulness of the use of armed force for the prevention or discontinuation of massive violations of human rights in a Member State.[102] There is still no consensus among Member States recognizing humanitarian intervention as an exception to the prohibition laid down in article 2 (4) of the Charter. Thus, the risk for a split between legality and legitimacy will remain in cases where the Security Council refuses to stop violations of human rights and humanitarian law on the basis of article 39 and 42 of the Charter. The practice of the Security Council to consider internal conflict a threat to international peace and security has been established since the conflict in Palestine in 1948 and Congo in 1961. Since the end of the Cold War, it seems to be widely accepted that extreme violence within a State can give rise to Chapter VII enforcement action. The Security Council has established a consistent practice with regard to Angola, Burundi, Liberia, Rwanda Sierra Leone, Somalia and Timor Leste in this regard. Therefore, the Security Council could build its application of the responsibility to protect on its practice that a threat to the peace can be considered in cases of mass atrocities, if it was in some way linked to a present or impending armed conflict or other destabilization of the security situation of a country or region.[103]

Therefore, a norm of customary international law might develop, ultimately filling the gap between legality and legitimacy. However, even then it remains necessary for the Security Council to fill the gap as well through systematic and predictable action on cases of massive human rights violations according to the Charter.

The concept of a collective obligation of the international community set out in paragraph 139 of the Summit Outcome receives some support from the International Law Commission (ILC) Draft Articles on State Responsibility, which determine that where the responsible State commits a serious breach of a peremptory norm of international law, other States have an obligation to cooperate to bring an end to that serious breach through lawful means.[104] The cooperation might be organized through an international organization, e.g. the United Nations, or through collective cooperation outside the United Nations. Furthermore, States must not recognize as lawful any situation created by the serious breach in question, neither formally nor through any act from which recognition would be implicit. However, the ILC itself recognizes that this aspect of its Draft Articles may go further than current

102 Randelzhofer, Article 2 (4), in: *Simma*, FN. 97, para. 53 et seq.

103 Frowein/ Krisch, Article 39, in: Ibid., para. 21.

104 ILC Draft Articles 40 and 41, U.N.-Doc. A/CN.4/L.600 of 11 August 2000. See for the drafting history and main content *James Crawford*, The International Law Commission's Articles on State Responsibility: Introduction, Text and Commentaries, Cambridge University Press, 2002.

customary law.[105] Unlike the Summit Outcome, the ILC limits this obligation to gross or systematic violations by the responsible State.

If the responsibility to protect was a legal norm, failure to implement its obligations would entail some legal sanctions. One could argue that inaction of the Security Council could trigger some kind of right or even duty of Member States to protest, but it is difficult to imagine how non-compliance of a political body could practically be challenged. The wording of the Outcome Document is hardly precise enough to allow holding Member States accountable for their inaction. Instead, the requirement of manifest failure may be used as a means to challenge the legality and timing of collective action by the international community.[106] The establishment of a duty of the Security Council to intervene in fulfillment of a responsibility to protect the population in a State would require an agreement on objective criteria for the establishment of manifest failure and the requirement of collective action in order to make it more difficult for Member States not to act. However, Member States did not include in the Summit Outcome the criteria for collective military action that have been developed to accelerate international decision making and make it more predictable.[107]

Finally, the responsibility to protect could be considered a more comprehensive concept comparable to the third generation rights like the right to development, the right to peace or the right to security. Those rights have been promoted in order to develop new approaches and priorities by summarizing and amending existing rights in a particular context where they might be more acceptable for States. The 'right', in this understanding, would be the flip side of the existing obligations of States to prevent and punish the listed crimes. Systematically, the responsibility to protect would fall into this category. As a 'third generation' right, the responsibility to protect might share some of the shortcomings of the other 'enabling' rights with regard to the monitoring of their implementation by States. It is also difficult to measure whether these rights actually contribute positively to the acceptance and implementation of the first and second generation rights they are designed to encompass. Furthermore, in international law, all rights are on the same level; there is no hierarchy of laws as in national law, where the constitution prevails over conflicting provisions in other bodies of law. The responsibility to protect would have the same status as, e.g. the right to access to court or the freedom of opinion and belief. This seems to be difficult to bring into line with the responsibility to protect as the ultimate objective of the United Nations as a whole.

Politically, the environment for the implementation of international human rights obligations is not very favorable in the present context of counter terrorism, reconfigurations of States and power, religious and ethnic conflict. In this context,

105 Commentary to Draft Article 2, para. (3), Yearbook of the International Law Commission, 2001, vol. II, Part Two.

106 *Stahn*, FN. 17, p. 99 et seq.

107 Ingo Winkelmann, "Responsibility to Protect": Die Verantwortung der Internationalen Gemeinschaft zur Gewährung von Schutz, in: *Pierre-Marie Dupuy et al.* (eds.), Völkerrecht als Wertordnung, Kehl, 2006, p. 449, 458 et seq.

any initiative that unites States behind common causes and with reference to human rights is welcome. At the same time, experience shows that States use the discussion about the broader common cause to avoid political pressure on their human rights record, which could undermine the implementation of the core human rights treaties. Furthermore, only implementation makes the difference for the individual person in the different countries. Member States tend to forget over the successful discussion and completion of new documents containing some agreement on principles and rights the painful and difficult work that will be required for their implementation and prefer to turn to new legislative projects rather than implementing the previous consensus.

3.4 Conclusions

While it is well understood that international law is considered the strongest form of international obligations among States, the history of failure of preventing genocide, war crimes and crimes against humanity during the last sixty years, notwithstanding applicable peremptory norms of international customary law to prevent and punish such crimes suggests that not much would be added by an additional norm as such. Instead, the responsibility to protect could, as a political concept, build the framework for the development of targeted action as viable political option for the United Nations in order to protect physically victims in situations of exceptionally grave violations of human rights and humanitarian law. The responsibility to protect could make existing legal obligations more effective and overcome the fundamental deficit in the current application of the international legal obligations. Ultimately, the responsibility to protect would aim at making military intervention a realistic threat to prospective violators of human rights and humanitarian law for that it does not have to be applied and thereby contribute to the prevention of such acts.

B. En vogue yet not in fashion? - Institutional practice of the Responsibility to Protect

1. Consideration of the responsibility to protect by the General Assembly

1.1 Considerations in general debates and within the work of main Committees

In their statements at the World Summit 2005,[108] 21 Member States referred to the responsibility to protect reflecting well the prevailing differences in the understanding of the agreement in the Summit Outcome document. While most of the supporters of the idea praised the compromise, the main opponents, namely Russia, India, Pakistan and Cuba, did not mention the agreement at all in their statements.[109]

While the Summit Outcome document 'stressed the need for the General Assembly to continue consideration of the responsibility to protect', Member States did not discuss the issue as such during subsequent sessions.

During the General Debate of the 61st Session, in September 2006, only 13 Member States, in their majority members of the European Union, referred to the responsibility to protect when reviewing the status of implementation of the Summit Outcome.[110] In the context of expressing concern at the situation in Darfur, speakers warned that the responsibility to protect had to be implemented. Australia, Canada, Denmark, Lichtenstein, Palau, Slovenia, Slovakia and Sweden agreed that the international community had a shared responsibility to protect people in Darfur. The United Kingdom considered the responsibility to protect in a wider context of the need for international cooperation and a responsibility of States for each other, as reflected best by the challenge of climate change. Luxemburg mentioned the responsibility to protect when referring to human rights and President Chirac of France expressed that 'building peace means shouldering responsibility to protect'.

108 All statements during the 2005 World Summit are available at http://www.un.org/webcast/summit2005/statements.html

109 See above A.1.

110 Statements during the General Debate of the 61st Session can be reviewed at http://www.un.org/webcast/ga/61/index.shtml

During the General Debate of the 62nd Session, at the end of September 2007, eight Member States mentioned the responsibility to protect in their statements.[111] From the African Group, only the Deputy Prime Minister of the Government of Lesotho, Archibald L. Lehohla, deplored that notwithstanding the agreement in the Summit Outcome document the Security Council was reacting late or not at all to protect populations from genocide, war crimes and crimes against humanity. Ambassador Hill of Australia repeatedly referred to the responsibility to protect in his statement, recalling the main content of the Summit Outcome document. He argued that the responsibility to protect provided necessary guidance to action on the situation in Darfur and other situations, where populations required protection. Other speakers deplored the lack of implementation of the agreement in the Summit Outcome document. Lithuania and Belgium encouraged the Secretary-General to follow up on the document and make it more 'operational'. In this context, Lichtenstein suggested to apply the responsibility to protect on the situation in Myanmar. The United Kingdom presented the improvement of the capacity of the United Nations to prevent the emergence of conflict as its 'vision' of the responsibility to protect.

In December 2007, the Fifth Committee of the General Assembly considered agenda item 128 on the Proposed programme budget for the biennium 2008-2009. The Fifth Committee is mandated to deal with administration and budget of the United Nations.[112] While its work could be considered mainly technical in nature, it includes the approval of spending for the Secretariat, peacekeeping operations and the daily functioning of the organization. Thus, the Committee can limit or delay the implementation of decisions by other organs and discussions often reflect political controversies that had not been resolved successfully.

In his report on Estimates in respect of special political missions, good offices and other political initiatives authorized by the General Assembly and/ or the Security Council,[113] the Secretary-General informed the General Assembly about his decision to appoint a Special Adviser for the Responsibility to Protect at the Assistant Secretary-General level in order 'to operationalize the concept and to develop the doctrine of the responsibility to protect'. The Secretary-General argued that such a position would complement the work of the Special Adviser on the Prevention of Genocide and should work closely with the latter to advance and consolidate the 2005 World Summit consensus and provide advice and recommendations in this regard. With a view to ensure effective coordination between the two Special Advisers, the Secretary-General requested additional staff for the Office of the Special Adviser on the Prevention of Genocide.[114]

111 Statements during the General Debate of the 62nd Session can be viewed at http://www.un.org/webcast/ga/62

112 See for details *Michael Peterson*, The UN General Assembly, Routledge, 2006, p. 63 et seq.

113 U.N.-Doc. A/62/512/Add.1 of 30 October 2007, para. 31.

114 Op. cit., para. 38.

Instead, the Fifth Committee adopted a resolution on the proposed programme budget for the biennium 2008-2009 in which it implicitly turned down the appointment of a Special Adviser on the Responsibility to Protect within the Office of the Special Adviser on the Prevention of Genocide.[115] In the course of the discussion, the representatives of Cuba, Egypt, India, Iran and Pakistan, rejected the proposal of the Secretary-General to appoint a Special Adviser on the Responsibility to Protect. They argued with different nuances that according to the Summit Outcome document, the General Assembly had a mandate to consider the responsibility to protect and since deliberations had not been concluded yet, the proposal, coming along as a budgetary and administrative issue, was considered premature.[116]

In March 2008, the Fifth Committee again discussed the appointment by the Secretary-General of a Special Adviser on the Responsibility to Protect. The representatives of Bangladesh, Cuba, Egypt, Iran, Nicaragua, Sudan and Venezuela requested clarification from the Secretariat on the recent appointment of a Special Adviser with focus on the responsibility to protect. The delegations argued that the respective proposal of the Secretary-General had not been approved by the Fifth Committee in December 2007 and, thus, the Secretariat disregarded the authority of the General Assembly.[117] Responding to the issues raised, the Secretariat argued that it did not understand the lack of approval of the proposed budget as a rejection, in general, by the General Assembly of the idea of a Special Adviser. Therefore, following consultations with different Member States, the Secretary-General had decided to make the appointment based on a temporary pro-bono agreement. All delegations taking the floor in the discussion following this reply expressed concern at the appointment procedure that did not involve the General Assembly as such notwithstanding previous discussions on the issue in December. In addition, Cuba, Egypt, Morocco, Nicaragua, Pakistan and Sudan stated that the General Assembly did not sufficiently discuss the agreement on the responsibility to protect in the Summit Outcome and Member States lacked consensus on its content and definition.[118]

On 18 April 2008, within the framework of his visit to the United States and the United Nations, Pope Benedict XVI addressed the General Assembly. In his statement he referred at length to the responsibility to protect, which he linked to the recognition of the unity of the human family and attention to the dignity of every man and woman. While only defined recently, he argued that it was present implicitly in the origins of the United Nations. The Pope stressed that the action of the international community and its institutions should never be considered an unwarranted imposition or a limitation of sovereignty, provided that it respected the principles underlying the international order. On the contrary, it was indifference or

115 See Press Release GA/AB/3835; U.N.-Doc. A/RES/62/238 of 20 February 2008, p. 4.

116 The discussion is reflected in Press Release GA/AB/3832.

117 See Press Release GA/AB/3836.

118 See Press Release GA/AB/3837.

failure to intervene that did the real damage. The Pope recalled that the principle of the responsibility to protect was considered by the ancient ius gentium as the foundation of every action taken by government with regard to those governed. When reference to the transcendence and natural reason was abandoned, like during the National Socialism in Germany, it threatened the objective foundation of the values inspiring and governing the international order and it undermined the cogent and inviolable principles the United Nations was based upon.[119]

On 22 May 2008, the General Assembly Plenary held a thematic debate on human security.[120] In his opening statement, the President of the General Assembly, Srgjan Kerim, expressed his view of a need for a new culture in international relations. In an interdependent world it was more important than before to embrace and enact principles of human security, international law and multilateral cooperation, human rights, responsibility to protect as well as protection of the environment and sustainable development. Prince El Hassan Bin Talal of Jordan observed that the concept of responsibility to protect in response to escalating violence remained more controversial and ideologically colored than 'such issues commonly are'. He expressed his opinion that the resolution of this debate was 'overdue'. There was no forward reason why sovereignty could not be shared to reflect the realities of an interdependent world. Egypt warned not to confuse human security with the responsibility to protect, if the latter was employed to justify intervention in domestic affairs between governments and their people. Human security needed to be an area that untied efforts, not a cause of conflict of interests or disagreement.

In the context of discussions of human rights violations in specific country situations in the Third Committee during the 61st and 62nd Session of the General Assembly, members of the Organization of the Islamic Conference recalled the principles of universality, objectivity and non-selectivity and stressed the need to strengthen the capacity of States in complying with human rights obligations through cooperation and genuine dialogue among civilizations, cultures and religions.[121]

Only at rare occasions, linked directly to the responsibility to protect, representatives of this group expressed their positions publicly. At a special public event organized by the OHCHR in New York on 28 April 2008, the representatives of Egypt expressed the view that the Summit Outcome document invited further dialogue and that no particular concept has crystallized so far. Following the line of argument of the Non-Aligned Movement, Sudan pointed out that there was no agreement among Member States on the interpretation of the Summit Outcome

119 Address to the General Assembly of the United Nations, http://www.un.org/webcast/pdfs/Pope_speech.pdf

120 See for details Press release GA/10711.

121 The position is best reflected in the statement by Ekemeleddin Ihsanoglu, Secretary General of the Organization of the Isalmic Conference at the High-level Segment of the 4th Session of the Human Rights Council, 12 March 2007, referring to the Baku Declaration adopted at the 33rd Session of the Islamic Conference of Foreign Ministers of 21 June 2006.

document and that the discussion on the responsibility to protect lead to ignore other concepts, including a holistic approach to the protection of civilians through development. Instead, the United Nations should encourage the political solution of conflicts.[122]

With a view to their public statements in the Third and Fifth Committee, Member States of the Non-Aligned Movement and the Organization of the Islamic Conference are perceived to oppose the operationalization of the responsibility to protect for fear of violations of their sovereignty. So far, this group of Member States was largely absent from discussions and conferences on the operationalization of the responsibility to protect or chose not to argue its case. The main positions of this group are known mainly indirectly from statements submitted in different United Nations bodies on issues related as well to the responsibility to protect, where representatives quote from the Final Document of the Summit Conference of the Non-Aligned Movement in Havana.[123] The document refers to the responsibility to protect in the context of 'Peaceful Settlement of Disputes and Non-Use or Threat of Use of Force' and states that

> [Heads of State and Government agreed to] remain seized of further deliberations in the UN on the responsibility to protect populations from genocide, war crimes, ethnic cleansing and crimes against humanity, bearing in mind the principles of the UN Charter and international law, including respect for the sovereignty and territorial integrity of States, non interference in their internal affairs, as well as respect for fundamental human rights.[124]

The position of the Member States of the Non-Aligned Movement becomes clearer when considering this statement in the context of the whole document, which repeated many of the arguments provided already during the negotiations of the Summit Outcome document. With regard to the follow-up to the 2005 World Summit in general, the Heads of State and Government only agreed to engage actively in the process to implement the commitments related to economic and social development and pursue issues that did not enter the final document to the extend they had desired, including disarmament, non-proliferation of weapons of mass destruction and arms control.[125] In their assessment of the international situation, the Heads of States and Government listed the continuing lack of resources and underdevelopment of the majority of countries among the main impediments to meet the challenges for economic development, peace and security and the enjoyment of human rights. They deplored that rich and powerful countries continued to exercise an inordinate influence on the direction of international relations.[126] The Movement reiterated that the Security Council must avoid resorting

122 Interactive Panel on "From manifest failure to collective action: Realizing the responsibility to protect", archived webcast available at http://www.un.org/webcast/SE2008.html

123 Final Document, 14th Summit Conference of Heads of State or Government of the Non-Aligned Movement, Havana, 16 September 2006, available at http://www.cohre.org/store/attachments/ RWP_NAM_2006_Havana_Summit_Final_Doc.pdf

124 Op. cit., para. 22.3.

125 Op. cit., para. 37.1 et seq.

126 Op. cit., para. 3 et seq.

to Chapter VII of the Charter as an umbrella addressing issues that did not pose a threat to international peace and security and that the Council should utilize fully other relevant provisions, including Chapter VI and VIII. Chapter VII should only be invoked as a measure of last resort. Any effort to increase the effectiveness of the United Nations to prevent conflict should be enhanced with the aim of achieving economic growth and sustainable development.[127] The Movement opposed any tendency to equate reform with greater empowerment of the Security-Council. Member States reiterated their concern at the perceived 'encroachment' by the Security-Council on the functions and powers of the General Assembly by addressing issues which fall traditionally within the competence of the General Assembly or by entering areas of norm-setting and establishing definitions.[128] The Heads of State and Government reiterated the role of the General Assembly in the maintenance of international peace and security and expressed grave concern at instances where the Security Council failed to address situations involving genocide, war crimes and crimes against humanity.[129] Humanitarian assistance should be kept distinct and independent of political or military action and be provided in accordance with the principles of humanity, neutrality and impartiality. The establishment of any peacekeeping operation should strictly observe the purposes and principles of the Charter and the principles that have evolved for those operations, including the consent of the parties, the use of force only in self-defense and impartiality. Peace keeping operations should not be used as a substitute for addressing the root causes of conflict.[130] With regard to human rights, the Heads of State and Government referred in particular to the right to development and underlined that human rights issues must be addressed through a constructive, dialogue-based approach, with respect for national sovereignty, territorial integrity, non-interference in internal affairs of States, impartiality, non-selectivity and transparency as guiding principles, taking into account the political, historic, social, religious and cultural particularities of each country.[131] They urged that in the discussion on human rights adequate attention was given to poverty, underdevelopment, marginalization, instability and foreign occupation, which could not be divorced from any meaningful discussion on human rights.[132]

At its Ministerial Conference in Teheran, the Movement confirmed its position on the responsibility to protect and to

> Remain seized of and active in further deliberations in the UN on the responsibility to protect populations from genocide, war crimes, ethnic cleansing and crimes against humanity, bearing in mind the principles of the UN Charter and international law, including respect for the

127 Op. cit., para. 38.7.
128 Op. cit., para. 42.
129 Op. cit., para. 45.5.
130 Op. cit., paras. 69.2, 69.5.
131 Op. cit., para. 234.2.
132 Op. cit., para. 234.6

sovereignty and territorial integrity of States, non-interference in their internal affairs, as well as respect for fundamental human rights.[133]

However, Egypt had tabled revised wording on the responsibility to protect that could only be rejected after intense discussions indicating the intention of some members of the Movement to revise the supporting position expressed in the Havana Document.[134]

China is perceived to be among the main opponents of the implementation of the agreement in the Summit Outcome document. Chinese diplomats deplored that their adherence to the principle of sovereignty was misinterpreted as disregard of the development of international law or an excuse to evade international responsibility. They argued that developing countries accepted international law developed in the West for hundreds of years as normative framework to conduct their international relations, because fundamental principles of the legal system reflected values they had been fighting for, including sovereignty, equality, democracy and self-determination. The international order was a result of the international reality, which was built upon a diversity of autonomous political entities. Even the Member States of the integrated Europe Union ultimately decided based on their national interests. Developments in Asia and Africa during the last 15 years confirmed the role of the State for any successful economic development and social progress. China accepted that the enjoyment of sovereign rights bore responsibility. States were accountable internally for the fulfillment of their international obligations. If a State breached international law, the rules of state responsibility would apply. Serious concerns arouse, where the internal situation of a State deteriorated. China opposed interventions of States invoking the responsibility to protect in situations, where alleged violations of general human rights obligations took place. To the extent that the responsibility to protect was limited by the United Nations Charter regarding collective action, the concept did not add anything to the existing situation. China supported international legal action, such as through the International Criminal Court (ICC), to stop atrocities and other forms of grave and massive violations of human rights.[135]

133 15th Ministerial Conference of the Non-Aligned Movement, Final Document, NAM 2008/Doc.1/Rev.2 of 30 July 2008, para. 17.2., available at http://embacuba.cubaminrex.cu/Default.aspx?tabid=8392

134 See Permanent Mission of the Arab Republic of Egypt to the United Nations, Proposed Language for the Section on "Promotion and Preservation of Multilateralism", CHAN/383/08/WA of 30 June 2008,

135 See e.g. *Hanquin Xue*, Chinese Observations on International Law. Speech at the International Criminal Law Network (ICLN), The Hague, 1 November 2006, available at http://www.icln.net

1.2 Conclusions

A preliminary review of the practice of the General Assembly regarding the responsibility to protect does not reveal much progress from the positions held by Member States during the negotiations of the Summit Outcome document. So far, no government or group of states indicated willingness to exercise leadership and propose a way forward for the General Assembly to continue consideration of the responsibility to protect. Since the 2005 World Summit, the number of Member States referring to the responsibility to protect in their statements in the general debate decreased constantly. Those Member States calling on the Secretary-General for leadership could not ensure that his initiative regarding a Special Adviser was approved by the General Assembly. The only country situations referred to during the general debate in the context of the responsibility to protect have been Darfur and Myanmar, but without suggesting any concrete elements of a continuum of steps that could be applied.

2. *Consideration of the responsibility to protect by the Security Council*

2.1 Consideration in thematic discussions

2.1.1 Consideration during discussions on the protection of civilians in armed conflict

Within the Security Council, Member States made public statements related to the responsibility to protect almost exclusively in the context of the protection of civilians in armed conflict.

The protection of civilians in armed conflict is an umbrella concept of humanitarian policies that integrates elements from international human rights and humanitarian law, military and security sectors and humanitarian assistance. Within the United Nations, the concept was introduced in the report of the Secretary-General on the situation in Africa, in 1998.[136] The Member States followed the recommendation of the Secretary-General to pay more attention to the monitoring and reporting on human rights during armed conflict and requested the Secretary-General to prepare a report with recommendations on how the Council could improve the physical and legal protection of civilians in armed conflicts.[137] Until

136 U.N.-Doc. S/1998/318 - A/52/871 of 13 April 1998.

137 S/PRST/1999/6 of 12 February 1999.

today, the Secretary-General has presented six reports to the Security Council.[138] In turn, the Council has issued three resolutions[139] and five Presidential Statements since 1999[140]. Since the adoption of the Summit Outcome document in September 2005, the Security Council held six open debates on the protection of civilians in armed conflict.

The Office for the Coordination of Humanitarian Affairs (OCHA) has led the development of an international policy framework for the implementation of the protection of civilians, in close cooperation with its humanitarian partner agencies and interested Member States. To this end, OCHA has developed an Aide memoire on the protection of civilians in armed conflict to assist the Security-Council and other UN departments in analyzing threats and developing adequate reaction. The Aide memoire was adopted by the Council as an annex to a Presidential Statement in 2001.[141]

After the Secretary-General had referred to the responsibility to protect in the conclusions of his fifth Report on the protection of civilians in armed conflict[142], many delegations touched on the issue in their statement during the open debate on 9 December 2005[143]. In his report, the Secretary-General expressed his pleasure at the emphasis of the Summit Outcome document of the responsibility to protect and recalled resolution 1296 (2000) in which the Council had reaffirmed its readiness to consider situations where the deliberate targeting of civilian populations and the committing of systematic, flagrant or widespread violations of international humanitarian or human rights law in situations of armed conflict might constitute a threat to international peace and security. Algeria, Brazil, China, Egypt, Mexico, Russia and South Africa recalled that the Summit mandated the General Assembly to continue consideration of the concept as there was no agreement on its parameters. They argued that it was premature for the Security Council to consider the issue. Argentina, Canada, Denmark, France, Greece, Italy, Rwanda, Slovakia and Switzerland supported suggestions for the Council to recall the agreement in the Summit Outcome document in the context of the protection of civilians as the document linked the responsibility to protect directly with collective action. Lichtenstein and Peru argued that the main obligation for the implementation of the responsibility to protect fell on the Security Council and, in order to meet their collective responsibility, the permanent members should refrain from submitting a veto on action aimed at preventing genocide, war crimes and crimes against humanity. Peru stressed that the responsibility to protect had to be viewed as a

138 Available at http://ochaonline.un.org/HumanitarianIssues/ProtectionofCiviliansinArmedConflict/DocumentsLibrary/tabid/1142/language/en-S/Default.aspx

139 U.N.-Doc. S/RES/1265 (1999) of 17 September 1999; S/RES/1296 (2000) of 19 April 2000.

140 U.N.-Doc. S/PRST/2002/6 of 15 March 2002; S/PRST/2002/41 of 20 December 2002; S/PRST/2003/27 of 15 December 2003; S/PRST/2004/46 of 14 December 2004.

141 S/PRST/2002/6 Annex of 15 March 2002.

142 Report of the Secretary-General on the protection of civilians in armed conflict, U.N.-Doc. S/2005/740 of 28 November 2005, p. 15.

143 See for the full records of the meeting S/PV.5319 and S/PV.5319 (Resumption 1).

concept that reflected the ultimate interest of national sovereignty of Member States, i.e. to safeguard human rights of their own citizens. The effective implementation of the responsibility to protect was important for the credibility of the United Nations. Tanzania argued that the consensus on the responsibility to protect was a useful basis for the further development and refinement of norms and practices related to the protection of civilians in armed conflict. There should be commonly agreed rules and benchmarks that would trigger collective action through regional organizations and the United Nations.

Prior to the public debate, the United Kingdom had circulated a draft resolution on the Protection of Civilians in Armed Conflict, which referred to the responsibility to protect in the preamble and the operational part of the text as follows[144]:

> PP 4. Recalling the 2005 World Summit Outcome Document, including its provisions regarding the responsibility to protect populations from genocide, war crimes, ethnic cleansing and crimes against humanity, and in this regard the responsibilities of individual Member States as well as the international community acting through the United Nations, including the Security Council [.]

> OP 6. Recalls the 2005 World Summit Outcome Document, and underlines the importance of its provisions regarding the responsibility to protect populations from genocide, war crimes, ethnic cleansing and crimes against humanity, including in this regard the responsibility of individual Member States as well as the international community acting through the United Nations, including the Security Council[.]

Negotiations on the resolution began in late November 2005, but Member States were unable to reach agreement on several aspects of the text, including the responsibility to protect. China and Russia, supported by three non-permanent members, promoted a cautious approach and considered the reference in the text premature. The responsibility to protect should be addressed by the General Assembly in more detail before it was included in a Security Council resolution. They were concerned that rapid interventions in exercise of the responsibility to protect could occur.[145] In early March, the negotiation process was moving forward a little, when China changed its position and indicated that it could accept a reference to the responsibility to protect in the text, if the exact same language of the Summit Outcome document was used. In addition, four of the new non-permanent members of the Council, who replaced the previous opponents, were in favor of a resolution endorsing the concept. Thus, the Russian position became increasingly isolated.[146] In the absence of any deadline facing the Council for action, the United Kingdom continued bi-lateral negotiations with Member States. Many Council members expressed frustration over the difficulties of agreeing on language for something that had been endorsed by the Heads of States and Governments only

144 Draft of 21 November 2005 at 10.07 a.m.

145 Security Council Report, Update Report No. 4, Protection of Civilians in Armed Conflict, 13 January 2006.

146 Security Council Report, Update Report No. 1, Protection of Civilians in Armed Conflict, 8 March 2006.

recently. Finally, the United Kingdom distributed a revised text of a draft resolution and on 28 April 2006, the Security Council passed resolution 1674 (2006), including the following operative paragraph on the responsibility to protect:

> Reaffirms the provisions of paragraphs 138 and 139 of the 2005 World Summit Outcome Document regarding the responsibility to protect populations from genocide, war crimes, ethnic cleansing and crimes against humanity [.][147]

During the public debate on the protection of civilians in armed conflict, on 28 June 2006, most Member States used the opportunity to express their satisfaction about the adoption by unanimity of resolution 1674 (2006).[148] Member States referring to the responsibility to protect mainly repeated their previous arguments. Those, who had supported a reference in the resolution from the outset, welcomed the 'endorsement'. China used the opportunity to clarify its understanding that the resolution reaffirmed a principle expressed in the Outcome Document which 'elaborated extensively on the concept'. However, this was 'not the same as the simple concept of the responsibility to protect, about which many countries continue to have concerns'. The new non-permanent members Ghana and Congo put on record their support for the responsibility to protect.

During the public debate on 4 December 2006, Under-Secretary-General for Humanitarian Affairs and Emergency Relief Coordinator, Jan Egeland, deplored that the international community was far away from seeing the responsibility to protect translate into predictable and adequate joint action to provide protection for all vulnerable groups of civilians irrespective of time, place and circumstances. He recalled that the United Nations had succeeded in providing security when joint action was taken by its Member States. This responsibility had to be depoliticized and become a truly shared interest of all Members of the Council. It had to transcend singular interests and become a core principle of humanity across civilizations.[149]

While statements followed pattern known from the previous debates, it should be noted that Russia joined China with the latter refining its previous position further by warning that it was not appropriate to expand, willfully interpret or even abuse the responsibility to protect as many Member States had expressed their concern and misgivings. Instead, all sides should abide by the agreed elements of the Summit Outcome document, i.e. its limitations to the four listed crimes. The United States repeated its reluctant statement from previous debates with hardly any changes in the wording and underlined that in situations where a government was unable or unwilling to protect its civilians, the international community had a complementary role to play. Denmark considered it irrelevant whether the responsibility to protect needed further consideration or not, since the basic political commitment not to allow another Rwanda or Srebrenica was a responsibility of all Members of the Council. Some delegations provided suggestions, which action the Council could take in particular situations. Japan suggested the development of a model matrix and

147 U.N.-Doc. S/RES/1674 (2006) of 28 April 2006, p. 2.

148 See for a detailed record S/PV.5476.

149 See S/PV.5577 and S/PV.5577 (Resumption 1).

argued that the Council should discuss how to best ensure the protection of civilians in situations like Darfur, where a serious gap remained between what the Government was willing and able to provide in terms of access and security and the real needs on the ground. Tanzania proposed that in situations where governments failed to protect their citizens or even caused insecurity themselves, the Security Council should hold them responsible and accountable. Finland suggested timely and adequate briefings by the Special Adviser on the Prevention of Genocide, the High Commissioner for Human Rights and the Emergency Relief Coordinator for the Council to prevent conflict. In this regard, Canada encouraged the Secretariat not to leave any room for ambiguity in its assessment of country situations and to provide the Security Council with concrete advice and recommendations.

During the public debate on 22 June 2007, all Member States repeated their previous positions. China requested the Council to refrain from invoking the concept of the responsibility to protect.[150] The representative of Mexico provided an appropriate summary of the debate, when he stated that

> '[d]espite the consensus reached in 2005, we cannot deny that an atmosphere of mistrust prevails over that subject. While some States see in the new principle the mere continuance of interventionist policies aimed at destabilizing political regimes, others promote its application in a selective manner, limiting its scope to cases significant for their foreign policy interests. For this reason, it is essential that States commit to reaching new agreements that give true content to such an important principle in an objective and impartial manner'.

In his concluding remarks, Under-Secretary-General for Humanitarian Affairs, John Holmes, suggested that the discussion should not focus too exclusively on the possible actions of last resort since there were many prior stages of helping countries to exercise their responsibility to protect.

In his Sixth Report, the Secretary-General highlighted the particular significance of the acceptance by all Member States of the responsibility to protect at the 2005 World Summit for the advances in the normative framework for the protection of civilians.[151] He announced that his Special Adviser on the Prevention of Genocide would contribute significantly to this achievement resulting in earlier and more decisive action to prevent and mitigate suffering of civilians in conflict areas. When addressing the open debate on 20 November 2007, the Secretary-General pledged to work with Member States and civil society to translate the responsibility to protect 'from word to deed', i.e. to ensure timely action when populations faced genocide, ethnic cleansing or crimes against humanity.[152]

Notwithstanding the presence of the Secretary-General, discussions followed the previous debates and no particular measure or initiative was proposed by the Member States.

150 See for a detailed record S/PV.5703.

151 Report of the Secretary-General on the protection of civilians in armed conflict, U.N.-Doc. S/2007/643 of 28 October 2007, p. 4.

152 See for a detailed record S/PV.5781 and S/PV.5781 (Resumption 1).

During the open debate on 27 May 2008, statements did not indicate that positions of Member States have shifted.[153] It was noteworthy, though, that many delegations mentioned the need to establish accountability for violations of human rights and humanitarian law as far as the Council was unable to prevent or halt such acts. In this context, delegations called on the international community to end impunity and support the work of the International Criminal Court. The Presidential Statement issued after the meeting did not refer to the responsibility to protect.[154]

2.1.2 Conclusions

Notwithstanding the policy framework developed by OCHA and the continuing process of open debates, the different understanding of the concept of the protection of civilians among departments, agencies, civil society and Member States prevails. The agreement in the Summit Outcome document on the responsibility to protect did not succeed in creating a momentum for a consensus on addressing more systematically situations of genocide, war crimes and crimes against humanity.

On the contrary, the close connection established with the protection of civilians became a liability for the operationalization of the responsibility to protect for various reasons.

First, the concept of the protection of civilians is both broader and narrower than the responsibility to protect. It is broader as far as it includes all violations of human rights and humanitarian law of a large number of the civilian population affected by armed conflict, while the responsibility to protect is limited to particular categories of crime. It is narrower as it limits the attention to violations occurring in armed conflict, while genocide and crimes against humanity could as well be committed outside such situations.

Second, the protection of civilians is linked to the broader idea of rights-based humanitarian action as a new approach to address human suffering. Therefore, the humanitarian principles of humanity, neutrality and independence apply to the concept and result in a difficult challenge on the ground to 'securing the protection of civilians that is demanded in law from all those responsible for enforcing these laws'[155]. While it is already a challenge for humanitarian agencies to encourage States and individuals to meet their humanitarian responsibilities to protect people while applying humanitarian principles, the responsibility to protect is based on the consensus that the international community must not remain neutral in situations, where genocide, war crimes and crimes against humanity might occur.

The responsibility to protect aims at introducing non-consensual military action against a Member State as a political option in the most extreme cases of abuse of civilians, while their government is manifestly failing to provide protection. To this

153 See S/PV.5898.
154 U.N.-Doc. S/PRST/2008/18 of 27 May 2008.
155 *Hugo Slim/ Luis Enrique Eguren*, Humanitarian Protection, A Guidance Booklet, p. 19

end, the responsibility to protect is understood as a continuum of steps, including prevention, protection and rebuilding. However, the application of humanitarian principles often prevents humanitarian actors from promoting military action in a particular country situation. Thus, the continuum of steps in implementation of the responsibility to protect cannot be applied within the political context of the protection of civilians as military action would, in fact, become more difficult to the disadvantage of vulnerable groups at risk as Member States would continue claiming to uphold humanitarian principles as an excuse for inaction.

Third, statements of the Under-Secretary-General for Humanitarian Affairs, the reports of the Secretary-General or the statements of Member States do not indicate a clear conceptual understanding of the relationship between the protection of civilians and the responsibility to protect. Instead, Member States differ significantly in their understanding of the content of the Summit Outcome document and the role of the Security Council in operationalizing the agreement.[156] Therefore, there is a risk that some Members of the Council will explore this link in favor of limiting the discussions on the responsibility to protect to the context of the protection of civilians and, in particular, to the responsibilities to prevent and to rebuild rather than the question of non-consensual military action. The Secretariat risks perpetuating this tendency through assisting the Council in its discussions. A precedent for this very problematic link was set when Under-Secretary-General for Humanitarian Affairs, John Holmes, in a briefing to the Security Council on his recent visit to Ethiopia, the Sudan and Somalia, claimed that humanitarian workers were in Sudan to help the Government fulfill its responsibility to protect its own citizens.[157] The relationship between the protection of civilians and the responsibility to protect needs to be clearly defined in this regard.

2.1.3 Consideration in other thematic discussions

In the context of other thematic discussions of the Security Council, Member States referred to the responsibility to protect in their statements. While no full account of such statements should be given, some examples will be listed below that might illustrate entry points for further consideration of the issue by the Council in the future.

In January 2007, the Security Council held a public debate on threats to international peace and security which marked the first official attendance of Secretary-General Ban Ki-Moon at a meeting of the Council.[158] In their statements,

156 In addition, there is a difference in understanding between France and the United Kingdom, i.e. the main supporters of the responsibility to protect. While the latter's approach is based on an interpretation of the Summit Outcome document, the former appears to reintroduce the 'devoir d'ingerence'. See e.g. Press Release SC/9454.

157 See S/PV.5792, p. 4

158 See for a full record S/PV.5615.

Members agreed on the need for the Council to pay more attention to conflict prevention and post-conflict peace-building. When referring to the responsibility to protect, Slovakia put it in context with the protection of civilians as part of preventive diplomacy efforts. Belgium sought a link with the close monitoring and implementation of arms embargoes in conflict areas and the impact on the civilian population. Only Peru mentioned the responsibility to protect in the context of a need for the Council to prevent the recurrence of genocide, war crimes and crimes against humanity. In his response, the Secretary-General listed the responsibility to protect among important achievements to build upon, which included as well the Peace Building Commission, the Human Rights Council and the Global Counter-Terrorism Strategy.

During a public debate on the role of the Security Council in supporting security sector reform, in February 2007, many delegations recognized the link between security, human rights and development. They concluded that security sector reform should be integrated within a broader context of improving governance.[159] However, only Panama referred to the responsibility to protect, which required the State to deliver security as a public service. The Security Council should support Member States in establishing a security sector that was able to fulfill that responsibility.

When the Council discussed post-conflict peace building, of all Members only Panama referred to the duty of the United Nations to assist States in their responsibility to protect populations in post-conflict situations.[160] The Netherlands used this occasion of a public debate to put on record their support of the responsibility to protect, but rather outside the considerations related to post-conflict peace building.

In his statement during the public debate on women, peace and security, in June 2008, Major-General Patrick Cammaert, former Division Commander of the United Nations Organization Mission to the Democratic Republic of the Congo (MONUC), left no space for diplomatic interpretation to the Members of the Security Council: The scale and brutality of sexual violence faced by women and girls in armed conflicts amounted to war crimes and crimes against humanity. Sexual violence had to be perceived as a threat to peace and security in the entire world, and in Africa in particular. Notwithstanding the many issues calling for the Council's attention, Member States had the responsibility to protect women and girls and to take real and effective measures to put an end to sexual violence.[161] However, from among the Members, only Viet Nam referred to the responsibility to protect and emphasized that States bear the primary responsibility to protect their own civilians and deal with violence against them, including sexual violence. The representative of Benin drew attention to mass rape as a weapon of war or as an instrument for ethnic cleansing or genocide. He suggested that the international community had to acquire the means to gain access to areas where such crimes are committed and must carry

159 See for a full record S/PV.5632
160 See S/PV.5895
161 See S/PV.5916

out investigations. The Council should be able to order special operations by virtue of the responsibility to protect.[162]

Resolution 1820 (2008) passed at the end of the debate reaffirmed the commitment to implement, inter alia, resolution 1674 (2006). The text of the preamble avoids mentioning the responsibility to protect using instead well-worn language by

> Recognizing that States bear primary responsibility to respect and ensure the human rights of their citizens, as well as all individuals within their territory as provided for by relevant international law,
>
> Reaffirming that parties to armed conflict bear primary responsibility to take all feasible steps to ensure the protection of affected civilians [.]

In the operative part of the resolution, the Security Council notes that rape and other forms of sexual violence can constitute a war crime, crime against humanity, or a constitutive act with respect to genocide.[163]

2.1.4 Conclusions

The agreement on the responsibility to protect at the Summit did not have positive impact on thematic discussions in the Security Council related to genocide, war crimes and crimes against humanity. No particular intention by Member States or regional groups appeared to refer to the responsibility to protect more systematically in order to benefit from the consensus for related areas of concern. Even those Member States which referred to the responsibility to protect in different discussions did not offer any concrete recommendations for implementation.

2.2 Consideration of the responsibility to protect in specific country situations

2.2.1 Darfur

In resolution 1706 (2006) concerning the situation in Sudan, the Council referred to the responsibility to protect indirectly when it recalled in a paragraph of the preamble

> its previous resolutions 1325 (2000) on women, peace and security, 1502 (2003) on the protection of humanitarian and United Nations personnel, 1612 (2005) on children in armed conflict, and 1674 (2006) on the protection of civilians in armed conflict, which reaffirms inter

162 See S/PV.5916 (Resumption)

163 See U.N.-Doc. S/RES/1820 (2008) of 19 June 2008.

> alia the provisions of paragraphs 138 and 139 of the 2005 United Nations World Summit outcome document [...][164]

When taking the floor after the vote on the resolution, the representatives of Argentina, Ghana and Tanzania pointed at the responsibility of the international community to protect the civilian population in Darfur.[165]

2.2.2 Somalia

In resolution 1814 (2008) concerning the situation in Somalia, the Security-Council

> Reaffirms its previous resolutions 1325 (2000) on women, peace and security, and 1674 (2006) and 1738 (2006) on the protection of civilians in armed conflict and stresses the responsibility of all parties and armed groups in Somalia to take appropriate steps to protect the civilian population in the country, consistent with international humanitarian, human rights and refugee law, in particular by avoiding any indiscriminate attacks on populated areas [.][166]

When presenting the Report of the Secretary-General to the Security Council, the Special Representative of the Secretary-General in Somalia, Ahmedou Ould-Abdallah, made reference to the responsibility to protect and its adoption at the World Summit and argued that the international community had a clearly mandated responsibility to become involved in a country where there are widespread violations of human rights and humanitarian law. He deplored that too much time was spent collecting data on the suffering of the Somali people while the real need was to be close to and protect the victims of armed violence, human rights abuses, drought and famine. While none of the Members of the Council picked up the suggestion, the representative of Somalia agreed that the Security Council had a responsibility towards the people of Somalia and a responsibility to protect the legitimate Government. This responsibility obliged the Council to look beyond the current limitations imposed by the security situation on the ground and reflect on a comprehensive solution.[167]

Notwithstanding these references to the responsibility to protect during the briefing, the resolution repeated wording used as well for other country situations, where the responsibility to protect had not been invoked. Thus, the text of the resolution must be interpreted as a rejection of the claims.

2.2.3 Conclusions

While little is known about the reasons for the Security Council to consider the responsibility to protect in one particular country-related resolution, but not the

164 U.N.-Doc. S/RES/1706 (2006) of 31 August 2006, p. 1

165 See for a detailed record S/PV.5519.

166 U.N.-Doc. S/RES/1814 (2008) of 15 May 2008, p. 5.

167 See S/PV.5858

other, when read in conjunction with the statements during the thematic discussions, some conclusions can be drawn.

The lack of unity in the Council or, in fact, the opposition of some Member States prevented the Council so far from applying the responsibility to protect on a specific country situation. At the same time, those Member States trying to further the agreement in the Summit Outcome document consider its application on a specific country situation important for any progress on operationalization. Therefore, it did not come as a surprise that the United Kingdom has tried to introduce references to the responsibility to protect in resolutions under its lead. However, at the same time, these resolutions did not reflect more than the common minimum denominator within the Council, i.e. the consideration of the responsibility to protect in the context of the protection of civilians and only within the limits of the exact wording of the Summit Outcome document. In this regard, the wording of resolutions 1674, 1706 and 1814 shows a regressive tendency within the Council to include wording related to the responsibility to protect. Resolutions 1706 and 1814 referred to resolution 1674 only in the context of the protection of civilians rather than as self-standing and cross-cutting consideration on the whole situation in Darfur and Somalia respectively. Only resolution 1706 contains an explicit reference to the Summit Outcome document.

This analysis is supported by examples of draft resolutions where wording related to the responsibility to protect has been deleted upon request of some Council members.[168] In the light of these resolutions, the wording of resolution 1814 (2008) should be considered as fully reflecting the deplorable status-quo within the Council related to the application of the responsibility to protect on country situations on its agenda.

3. *Consideration of the responsibility to protect in the work of the Secretariat*

3.1 Public statements by the Secretary-General and senior officials

Former Secretary-General Kofi Annan referred repeatedly to the responsibility to protect in his statements on the situation in Darfur. In a very strong message to the Security Council in a public meeting on 11 September 2006, he argued that after the agreement on the responsibility to protect at the World Summit there was no time for middle-ground of half-measures or further debate as lessons were either learned or not and principles were either upheld or scorned.[169] In December 2006, he pointed

168 The draft e.g. of resolution 1769 (2007), dated 30 July 2007, contained a reference to the World Summit Outcome document following the title of resolution 1674 (2006) listed in para. 4 of the preamble, see U.N.-Doc. S/RES/1769 (2007) of 31 July 2007, p. 1.

169 See S/PV.5520, p. 3.

out to journalists the collective and individual responsibility of the Government of Sudan for its failure to meet its responsibility in Darfur. One day later, in an address to mark International Human Rights Day, Kofi Annan deplored that despite the adoption of the responsibility to protect, reports from Darfur on the destruction of hundreds of villages continued. In particular, he turned against those Member States who tried to depict the responsibility to protect as in imperialistic conspiracy against developing countries.[170]

In his report on the implementation of decisions from the World Summit he did not inform about specific activities of the Secretariat related to the responsibility to protect, though.[171]

Very early in his tenure, Secretary-General Ban Ki-Moon called on Member States to give 'real meaning' to the responsibility to protect as agreed upon at the 2005 World Summit by making it operational through practical steps.[172] Later he declared the operationalization of the responsibility to protect one of his priorities.[173]

As a visible step, he announced publicly his intention to appointing a Special Adviser on the Responsibility to Protect.[174] Even though he had informed the Security Council of his intention already in a letter dated 31 August 2007[175], the President of the Council responded only on 7 December that the Members took note of the appointment[176]. Following controversial discussions with the General Assembly on the budget, the Secretary-General finally appointed Edward Luck Special Adviser, 'who will focus on the responsibility to protect'.[177] At a press briefing, the spokesperson explained that Mr. Luck's primary role would be conceptual development and consensus building, to assist the General Assembly to continue consideration of the issue.[178]

With regard to country situations, the Secretary-General referred to the responsibility to protect for the first time in January 2008 when he reminded the Government as well as the political and religious leaders of Kenya of their legal and moral responsibility to protect the lives of innocent people, at the beginning of the post-election crisis in the country.[179] In April, he reminded Israel of its responsibility

170 Reflected in: Address by Mr. Kofi Annan on receiving the MacArthur Award for International Justice, New York, 20 March 2008.

171 Implementation of decisions from the 2005 World Summit Outcome for action by the Secretary-General, U.N.-Doc. A/60/430 of 19 October 2005.

172 Secretary-General's message on the 13th anniversary of the Rwanda Genocide, 9 April 2007.

173 Secretary-General's address to the Parliament of Rwanda, 29 January 2008.

174 Secretary-General's message to UNU-ICG Conference on the Prevention of Mass Atrocities, 10 October 2007. He had first indicated his consideration of such a step in his remarks at the opening of the exhibition "Lessons from the Rwanda Genocide", 30 April 2007.

175 U.N.-Doc. S/2007/721 of 7 December 2007.

176 U.N.-Doc. S/2007/722 of 7 December 2007.

177 Press Release SG/A/1120, BIO/3963.

178 Press Release, Spokesperson's Noon Briefing, 21 February 2008.

179 Press Release SG/SM/11356. See for a more detailed review of the implementation of the responsibility to protect in the Kenya crisis, below C.3.2.

to protect civilians under international humanitarian law during military operations in Gaza.[180]

In July 2008, the Secretary-General used the occasion of a conference in Berlin to clarify his understanding of the responsibility to protect.[181] In his presentation, he underscored his deep and enduring personal commitment to the responsibility to protect. He explained that it was a concept, not yet a policy, which rested on three pillars: (1) In the Summit Outcome document, governments unanimously affirmed the primary and continuing legal obligations of States to protect their populations. (2) The Summit underscored the commitment of the international community to assist States in meeting these obligations. With a view of the magnitude of the crimes involved, the goal must be to assist States in early, preventive steps and not just to react when atrocities unfold. (3) States accepted their responsibility to react in a timely and decisive manner to help protect populations from the four listed crimes. The response should be early and flexible and involve the whole range of United Nations tools as provided for in Chapter VI, VII and VIII of the Charter. The Secretary-General described his conception of the responsibility to protect as 'narrow but deep'. Its scope was narrow as it focused only on the four crimes and violations provided for in the Summit Outcome document. At the same time, the response to those crimes should be deep and involve the whole range of prevention and protection activities of the United Nations. In the understanding of the Secretary-General, the responsibility to protect did not alter but reinforced the legal obligations of Member States with regard to the use of force or the principle of sovereignty. The Secretary-General argued that if Member States could agree to act collectively in cases of mass atrocities, others might be deterred from committing such atrocities as well as from taking extra-legal unilateral action. The Secretary-General announced that his Special Adviser would work on the conceptual, institutional and political dimension of the responsibility to protect, sharing an office with the Special Adviser on the Prevention of Genocide. Late in 2008, the Secretary-General intended to report to the General Assembly on his proposed approach and the challenges posed by the Summit Outcome document.

Since the 2005 World Summit, different senior officials of the United Nations referred to the responsibility to protect in public statements. As mentioned already above, the responsibility to protect was linked by the Under Secretary-General for Humanitarian Affairs to the discussion on the protection of civilians in armed conflict and invoked by the Special Representative of the Secretary-General in Somalia. Other senior officials participated on behalf of the organization in public conferences on the issue.

The High Commissioner for Human Rights, Louise Arbour, took a particular visible position, when she argued at the occasion of a lecture at Trinity College in

180 Statement Attributable to the Spokesperson for the Secretary-General on the Latest Violence in the Gaza Strip, 28 April 2008; Statement Attributable to the Spokesperson for the Secretary-General on the latest violence in southern Israel and Gaza, 5 June 2008

181 Press Release SG/SM/11701.

Dublin that an emerging doctrine of responsibility to protect carried important implications for human rights theory and practice. The community of nations was progressively defining a framework for the prevention of, and protection against, state-sponsored slaughter. She interpreted the responsibility to protect as configuring a permanent duty to protect individuals against abusive behavior. The international community held no longer a discretionary right to intervene, but was burdened with the responsibility to take action under the doctrine of responsibility to protect.[182]

3.2 The internal work of the Secretariat

Following the 2005 World Summit, based on the mentioning of his Office in the Summit Outcome document in the context of the responsibility to protect,[183] delegations, civil society and United Nations colleagues approached the Office of the Special Adviser on the Prevention of Genocide with a view to explore options for the involvement of the Secretariat in the future implementation of the agreement on the responsibility to protect. The Special Adviser initiated a discussion within the Executive Committee on Peace and Security (ECPS) on how to move the agreement forward. The ECPS decided to set up an informal Working Group to identify and develop a repertoire of measures within the existing mandates and responsibilities of United Nations departments and agencies that could assist Member States in fulfilling effectively their responsibility to protect.

The objective of the Working Group was based on the assumption that within the agreement on the responsibility to protect in the Summit Outcome, consensual and non-consensual measures were considered a continuum where the former would reduce the need for or intensity of, the latter. A focus on military intervention would be likely to inspire resistance from Member States and limit the possibility to mobilize political will to apply the agreement at an early stage. The Secretariat could play an important role in informing and assisting Member States in their considerations by identifying institutional resources and responsibilities that may help Member States to meet their individual and collective responsibility to protect.

The Working Group tried to collect contributions from all members of ECPS based on a table identifying possible impact, timeframe and challenges for each measure. The repertoire of measure was classified along the three categories reflected in the wording of the Outcome Document, i.e. diplomatic, humanitarian and other peaceful means. Working Group members agreed that from the whole range of possibilities to protect groups at risk, it was required to identify those measures particularly suited to prevention, reaction and rehabilitation in the face of genocide, war crimes, ethnic cleansing and crimes against humanity.

182 United Nations Press Release, High Commissioner addresses Dublin's Trinity College on responsibility to protect, 29 November 2007.

183 Paragraph 140 of the Summit Outcome document reads: "We fully support the mission of the Special Adviser of the Secretary-General on the Prevention of Genocide."

In its report to ECPS, the Working Group concluded that the political will of Member States to apply the responsibility to protect to specific country situations would depend to a great extend on available options short of military intervention. Difficulties arouse in identifying focused, short-term measured designed to address specifically the prevention of genocide, war crimes and crimes against humanity. Finally, there was a need to establish a common understanding of the responsibility to protect, the agreement in the Summit Outcome document and the possible role of the Secretary-General within the Secretariat and United Nations funds and agencies.

After the submission of the report, discussions continued in preparation of a meeting of the Secretary-General's Policy Committee. OCHA expressed concern that, in the current political climate, the discussion about the responsibility to protect might jeopardize some aspects of the humanitarian agenda and argued that its application should be limited to 'high-threshold instances'. Others, including OHCHR, pointed out that the specific prevention based language used in the Outcome Document could not exclude the application of the responsibility to protect and restrict it from the outset to exceptional cases as this interpretation would neutralize any impact prior to a full-fledged crisis.

After holding three meetings of the Policy Committee on the responsibility to protect, the Secretary-General decided on a way forward notwithstanding remaining differences within United Nations agencies, funds and departments. As indicated in the presentation of the Secretary-General in Berlin, the main steps will include the integration of the responsibility to protect and the prevention of genocide in a single office based on the existing resources. The establishment of a specialized Committee should ensure inter-departmental and agency cooperation on the responsibility to protect. Finally, consultations with Member States, civil society and within the Secretariat, funds and agencies will continue. The General Assembly will be able to review the approach when discussing the report of the Secretary-General, presumably in early 2009.

3.3 Conclusions

While Kofi Annan invoked the responsibility to protect forcefully in public statements, in particular related to the situation in Darfur, he neither provided guidance to Member States on the implementation of their agreement nor requested the Secretariat to discuss or prepare his possible role in a future process. In addition, his public statements left open which indicators or standards he selected for his application and did not include any proposals of a continuum of steps that Member States could have taken in order to mitigate the situation.

Secretary-General Ban Ki-Moon made the implementation of the responsibility to protect one of the priorities of his tenure. So far, he has been very cautious in addressing specific country situations in this context or in revealing a possible role of the Secretariat in the future. This task will mainly fall on his Special Adviser. At the same time, many questions raised in the report of the ECPS Working Group remain unanswered. The speech in Berlin only partly clarified the interpretation of the responsibility to protect for the future work of the Secretariat in the context of previous statements that did not indicate a coherent application of the concept.

In particular, the limited resources available to the United Nations and the international community cannot address effectively the root causes of genocide, war crimes and crimes against humanity across the globe. Therefore, the United Nations will have to establish a mechanism to react quickly to situations, where imminent or ongoing violence might lead to situations described in the Summit Outcome. Serious shortcomings prevail in the development and application of measures to address imminent or ongoing violence that could constitute genocide, war crimes and crimes against humanity.

In January 1994, General Dallaire, commander of the United Nations Assistance Mission for Rwanda (UNAMIR), sent a code cable to New York on information he had received on the registration of Tutsi and major arms caches and requested the authority to take action to prevent the possible killing.[184] While the response from New York became famous for its restrictive interpretation of UNAMIR's mandate, it is also questionable whether any coherent set of measures could have been proposed and implemented with the aim to prevent the mass killings. Unfortunately, even after the traumatic experience, the United Nations would hardly be better prepared today than in1994.

Ultimately, the implementation of the responsibility to protect by the Member States will require decisive leadership by the Secretary-General based on the experience and technical ability of the Secretariat and United Nations agencies and funds to provide options for policy decisions on country situations.

4. Consideration of the responsibility to protect in the work of the Human Rights Council

4.1 The High-Level Mission on Darfur and its follow-up

In December 2006, during its fourth special session on the human rights situation in Darfur, the Human Rights Council decided to dispatch a High-Level Mission to assess the human rights situation in Darfur and the needs of the Sudan in this regard.[185] The responsibility to protect was not invoked during the discussion.[186]

184 See for details on these events *Power*, FN. 62, p. 335 et seq.

185 See for details Report on the Fourth Special Session of the Human Rights Council, U.N.-Doc. A/HRC/S-4/5 of 22 January 2007.

186 See United Nations Press Release, Human Rights Council opens special session on Darfur, 12 December 2006; Special session of Human Rights Council on Darfur continues General Debate, 12 December 2006.

The High-Level Mission determined that international humanitarian and human rights law was the most appropriate framework for addressing the central issue of the effective protection of civilians in Darfur and decided 'to employ an analysis drawn from the responsibility to protect'.[187] The Mission argued that Sudan joined in the adoption of the World Summit Outcome, explicitly accepting the responsibility to protect. In addition, Sudan ratified numerous human rights treaties and signed political agreements that, according to the Mission, together with national legislation and policies, 'underpin this responsibility'.[188]

When reviewing Sudan's action regarding the responsibility to protect, the Mission noted the pattern of large-scale attacks in Darfur and observed that they were characterized by a coordination of operations between Sudanese armed forces and government-supported militia and by grave violations of human rights and humanitarian law. With regard to the well-known pattern of rape of women around Internally Displaced People (IDP) camps, the Mission concluded that little has been done to diminish the threat or investigate cases reported. Furthermore, the Mission reported large-scale arbitrary arrests of Darfurians and torture, inhuman and degrading treatment by National Security and Military Intelligence.[189] With regard to the violations of economic, social and cultural rights, the Mission found that the widespread displacement and the massive destruction of villages, property and lands has limited further access to food and water, which was further hampered by the obstruction of humanitarian access and a general shrinking of humanitarian space.[190]

The Mission reviewed the international community's responsibility to protect, starting with the activities of the Security Council, including the International Commission of Inquiry on Darfur and the passing of key resolutions. The list included action by other United Nations bodies and agencies such as the Human Rights Council, OHCHR, treaty-bodies and humanitarian organizations as well as action by the African Union. The Mission concluded that as important as these steps may have been, they have not proven adequate in ensuring effective protection on the ground and gross violations of human rights and humanitarian law continued across the region.[191]

Based on an assessment of the most pressing needs in Darfur and previous recommendations by different human rights mechanisms that remained unimplemented, the Mission concluded that the Government of Sudan has manifestly failed to protect the populations of Darfur from large-scale international crimes and has itself orchestrated and participated in these crimes. As such, the obligation of the international community to exercise its responsibility to protect has become evident and urgent.[192]

187 Report of the High-Level Mission on the situation of human rights in Darfur pursuant to Human Rights Council decision S-4/101, U.N. Doc. A/HRC/4/80 of 9 March 2007, p. 2.

188 Op. cit., para. 19 et seq.

189 Op. cit., para. 38 et seq.

190 Op. cit., para. 54 et seq.

191 Op. cit., para. 67

192 Op. cit., para. 76

When the High-Level Mission presented its Report, controversy erupted about the legitimacy of its findings and the cooperation by the Government of Sudan, since the Mission had not been able to enter Sudan. The application of the responsibility to protect was not discussed in any detail.[193] Finally, the Members of the Council agreed to 'take note' of the report of the High-Level Mission which allowed the controversy about its findings and recommendations to prevail without preventing the adoption of a decision.

The Human Rights Council decided to convene a group of seven mandate holders to work with the Government of Sudan on the implementation of the different resolutions and recommendations by human rights mechanisms that had been issued earlier on the situation in Darfur.[194] Even though the text of the decision was adopted without a vote, the statements of delegations reflected the difficulties encountered by the European Union and the African Group to agree on any follow-up to the High-Level Mission report.[195] The Human Rights Council requested the Group to continue its work for six month, to submit an interim report to the session of the Council in September 2007 and a final report to the following session in December 2007.[196]

The Expert Group agreed to work in a transparent manner with the Government of Sudan and others within the international community on identifying the obstacles to the implementation of previous resolutions and to prioritize recommendations and define reachable steps that are tangible for the victims in the short and medium term.[197] The Group interpreted its task as a forward-looking exercise rather than an assessment of past activities undertaken by the Government of Sudan.[198] Based on the documentation examined, the Group identified four priority areas, i.e. human rights protection, humanitarian access, accountability and justice, and monitoring of implementation of recommendations. For each priority area, the experts selected a number of recommendations, identified steps that could be considered indicators for their implementation and assessed the length of time, between three and twelve month, needed for their implementation. The respective matrix was shared with the Government of Sudan, which agreed with a substantial number of recommendations

193 The representatives of the UK and Canada referred to the responsibility to protect in their statements as an argument for the need for the Council to agree on concrete measures on Darfur, see United Nations Press Release; Human Rights Council discusses report of High-Level Mission on Situation of Human Rights in Darfur, 16 March 2007.

194 Resolution 4/8, Follow-up to decision S-4/101 of 13 December adopted by the Human Rights Council at its fourth special session entitled "Situation of human rights in Darfur", of 30 March 2007, see Report to the General Assembly on the Fourth Session of the Human Rights Council, U.N.-Doc. A/HRC/4/123 of 12 June 2007, p. 18.

195 See for details United Nations Press Release, Human Rights Council adopts seven resolutions and two decisions including text on Darfur, 30 March 2007.

196 Resolution OM/1/3 of 20 June 2007.

197 Report on the situation of human rights in Darfur prepared by the group of experts [...]. U.N.-Doc. A/HRC/5/6 of 8 June 2007, para. 7.

198 Op. cit., para. 9.

although it remained unclear sometimes what specific steps it would undertake for their implementation.[199]

With regard to the three main areas of concern identified by the High-Level Mission, the Government of Sudan agreed to short-term measures for immediate implementation, including e.g. to issue and enforce clear orders to armed forces and any militias under its control on the protection of civilians under humanitarian law, to publicly acknowledge and condemn violence against women, and to issue and enforce instructions to law enforcement agencies against torture, arbitrary arrest and enforced or involuntary disappearances.[200]

In its interim report, the Expert Group reported that it had decided not to present a detailed evaluation of the current status of implementation of specific recommendations in order to give the Government of Sudan the maximum possible time to undertake initiatives and report back to the Commission.[201] The experts noted certain discrepancies between information provided by the Government of Sudan and other sources. The group concluded that, in any case, it was not in a position to report that clear impact on the ground had been identified so far and deplored that certain short-term recommendations were not addressed by the Government of Sudan at all.[202]

In its final report, the Expert Group highlighted that the process of cooperative engagement with the Government of Sudan worked well in procedural terms, while in terms of substance few recommendations had been fully implemented or have had any tangible impact on the ground. Several recommendations that had been prioritized as short-term and could have been implemented within three months, as they did not require lengthy administrative processes or additional resources had not been implemented. These recommendations included the three priority areas identified by the High-Level Mission. The Group of Experts acknowledged the activities undertaken by the Government, but expressed concern that these efforts did not lead to an improvement of the overall situation of human rights in Darfur. The group recommended that the Human Rights Council continued the process of review in accordance with the time frames and indicators for assessing implementation as developed by the Group.[203]

In its consideration of the report, the Human Rights Council adopted without a vote a resolution acknowledging the efforts of the Government of Sudan to implement the recommendations and expressing concern that the implementation of many recommendations has not been fully completed.[204] The text of the resolution

199 Op. cit., para. 11 et seq.

200 Op. cit., Annex I.

201 See United Nations Press Release, Human Rights Council considers human rights situations that require its attention, 24 September 2007.

202 Interim report on the situation of human rights in Darfur prepared by the group of experts mandated by the Human Rights Council, U.N.-Doc. A/HRC/6/7 of 22 September 2007.

203 Final report on the situation of human rights in Darfur prepared by the group of experts […], U.N.-Doc. A/HRC/6/19 of 28 November 2007.

204 U.N.-Doc. A/HRC/6/L.51 of 13 December 2007.

was a political compromise that has to be read in conjunction with the resolution extending the mandate of the Special Rapporteur on the situation of human rights in Sudan, in which the Special Rapporteur was requested, inter alia, to ensure effective follow-up and to foster the implementation of the remaining short-term and the medium-term recommendations identified in the first report of the Group of Experts.[205] While the European Union did not succeed in extending the mandate of the Group of Experts, the African Group 'respected the specific desires of countries to get support and, thus was encouraging the extension of the mandate'.[206]

In her report to the seventh session of the Human Rights Council on the situation of human rights in Sudan, the Special Rapporteur referred to the recommendations of the Expert Group in general terms, but did not offer a detailed review.[207] Following the presentation of the report, the Council adopted without a vote a resolution in which it

> Stresses the primary responsibility of the Government of the Sudan to protect all its citizens, including all vulnerable groups; [...]
>
> Urges the Government of the Sudan to continue and intensify its efforts to implement the recommendations identified by the Group of Experts, in accordance with the specified time frames and indicators [.][208]

Using the indicators and timelines developed by the Group of Experts, the Special Rapporteur provided a comprehensive assessment of the Government's activities to implement short-term and medium-term recommendations and their impact reported from the ground to the ninth session of the Human Rights Council.[209] The Special Rapporteur concluded that recommendations have not been implemented fully while the time-frame for action by the Government had elapsed on 20 June 2008. In any case, the measures of implementation have not had any impact as attacks on civilians and civilian objects by the Government forces or allied militias continued and the civilian population remained largely unprotected throughout Darfur. The Special Rapporteur recommended that the Human Rights Council continued the process of review in accordance with the indicators and consider further action to protect and promote the human rights of people in Darfur.

205 U.N.-Doc. A/HRC/6/L.50 of 13 December 2007.

206 Sameh Shoukry (Egypt), as reflected in United Nations Press Release, Human Rights Council extends mandates of Experts on the Internally Displaced Persons, Sudan and the Freedom of Religion and Belief, 14 December 2007.

207 Report of the Special Rapporteur on the situation of human rights in the Sudan, Sima Samar, U.N.-Doc. A/HRC/7/22 of 3 March 2008, p. 10 et seq.

208 Resolution 7/16, see Draft report of the Council, U.N.-Doc. A/HRC/7/L.11 of 28 March 2008, p. 60 et seq.

209 Report prepared by the Special Rapporteur on the situation of human rights in the Sudan on the status of implementation of the recommendations compiled by the Group of Experts mandated by the Human Rights Council in resolution 4/8 to the Government of the Sudan pursuant to Human Rights Council resolution 6/34, U.N.-Doc. A/HRC/9/13/Add.1 of 2 September 2008.

During the interactive dialogue with the Special Rapporteur, Sudan, Egypt on behalf of the African Group, Algeria and Cuba expressed their opposition to an extension of the mandate.[210] After intense negotiations between the European Union and the African Group, the Human Rights Council extended the mandate of the Special Rapporteur for six month after passages quoting from the report of the Special Rapporteur had been deleted from the text.[211] The Special Rapporteur was requested to further ensure the follow-up the implementation of the remaining recommendations of the Group of Experts.

4.2 Conclusions

The attempt of the High-Level Mission to apply the responsibility to protect to its assessment of the human rights situation in Darfur constitutes a very important example for the opportunities related to this approach. Even though its methodology was not set out in detail, it appears that an assessment of the situation could be made based on reports submitted to or by other United Nations entities, such as the Independent Inquiry Mission to Darfur and the regular reports by United Nations Missions and experts. In its follow-up, the expert group set an important precedent for the definition and application of measures of short-term, medium-term and long-term prevention in situations of ongoing large-scale violence, their timelines and possible indicators. Many of the recommendations could be adapted easily to other situations of imminent or ongoing large-scale violence with the alleged involvement of the Government.

At the same time, the Human Rights Council proved to be too weak as a body to carry through the full implementation of its recommendations. In addition to unity it lacked any effective sanctions it could have applied. Therefore, for the responsibility to protect to be applicable, other United Nations organs, in particular the Security Council and the Secretary-General need to support the implementation of such recommendations by integrating them into their own work. The continuum of measures within the responsibility to protect requires a joint approach without sharp edges in order to avoid situations falling only within a particular mandate.

5. *Advocacy of the responsibility to protect by civil society*

Since the Outcome Document was published, civil society and academia discussed the opportunities for the United Nations to operationalize the agreement on the responsibility to protect. Through the discussion, two main groups of supporters

210 United Nations Press Release, Special Rapporteur on Situation of Human Rights in Sudan presents report to Human Rights Council, 16 September 2008.

211 See for details U.N.-Doc. A/HRC/9/L.2/Rev.1 of 24 September 2008.

could be identified. So far, there is no noticeable group openly opposing the implementation of the agreement, while many academics expressed skepticism about its maximum capacity to improve the ability of the United Nations to address genocide, war crimes and crimes against humanity.[212]

Notwithstanding the compromise in the Summit Outcome, in particular former members of the ICISS and supportive Member States claimed that the World Summit had adopted mainly the concept presented in the ICISS Report of 2001. Most prominently, the former co-chair of the ICISS, Gareth Evans, has been working tirelessly since the World Summit to advocate the full implementation of the 'doctrine' of responsibility to protect. In countless lectures, articles and public statements he has acknowledged the difficulties deriving from lack of capacity and lack of political will to implement the responsibility to protect and tried to keep 'false friends', e.g. the United Kingdom claiming that the war in Iraq was fought to protect the people of Iraq from Saddam Hussein's regime, at arm's length.[213] He referred to a 'risk of backsliding' when pointing out the skepticism within Asian states regarding steps to operationalize the agreement.[214] He has considered the development of criteria for the application of non-consensual military force an 'important piece of unfinished business'.[215] In more recent statements, he repeated his view that the responsibility to protect was not about military action, but prevention, including early prevention.[216] At the same time, Evans reiterated that the responsibility to protect should not be linked to other tasks as it was developed specifically for a precisely defined set of situations, i.e. those actually or potentially involving large-scale killing, ethnic cleansing or similar abuse.[217]

212 See e.g. *Alex de Waal*, No Such Thing as Humanitarian Intervention. Why We Need to Rethink How to Realize the 'Responsibility to Protect' in Wartime, The Harvard International Review, 2008, http://www.harvard.edu/articles/1482/; very skeptical, but under the assumption that the responsibility to protect would entail a legal obligation to intervene *Steven Groves*, The U.S. Should Reject the U.N. 'Responsibility to Protect' Doctrine, Backgrounder No. 2130, 1 May 2008.

213 See Gareth Evans, From Humanitarian Intervention to the Responsibility to Protect, Keynote Address to Symposium on Humanitarian Intervention, University of Wisconsin, Madison, 31 March 2006, available at http://www.crisisgroup.org/home/index.cfm?id=4521&l=1.

214 See Gareth Evans, Making Idealism Realistic: The Responsibility to Protect as a New Global Security Norm, Address to launch Stanford MA Program in International Policy Studies, Stanford University, 7 February 2007, loc. cit.

215 See Gareth Evans, Responsibility to Protect in 2007: Five Thoughts for Policy Makers, Presentation to Panel Discussion on The Responsibility to Protect: Ensuring Effective Protection of Populations under Threat of Genocide and Crimes Against Humanity, United Nations, New York, 13 April 2007, loc. cit.

216 See Gareth Evans, The Responsibility to Protect and the Use of Military Force, Presentation to Seminar on International Use of Force, World Legal Forum, The Hague, 11 December 2007, loc. cit.

217 Gareth Evans, in: Conference Report, SEF Symposium 2007, The Responsibility to Protect: Progress, Empty Promise or a License for Humanitarian Intervention?, Bonn, 2008, p. 15 et seq.

Another former member of the ICISS, Ramesh Thakur, tried to focus the discussion on implementation of the ideas and findings of the Commission. He argued that responsibility to protect pointed a way towards ensuring that intervention, when it did take place, was done properly. Since, on its own, the deterrent effect of prosecution had not always been enough to prevent atrocities, the responsibility to protect provided for the option of regional or international intervention as ultima ratio. The proposal had to be seen in a broader context of the role of the United Nations in preventing and halting massive violations of human rights. He recalled that, according to the Charter, the United Nations was not a pacifist organization. Rules-based multilateral intervention was preferable to ad-hoc unilateral interventions and every effort had to be made for the Security Council to exercise and not abdicate its responsibility. Thakur cautioned that main industrialized countries found it beyond their imagination to be subject to an intervention based on the responsibility to protect and, thus, could not appreciate the concern of developing countries to become subject of an intervention by tomorrow's moral majority. Similarly, international criminal justice would remain suspect for the developing countries as long as no major western leader was prosecuted as well.[218]

Public advocacy for the responsibility to protect by former members of the ICISS is an indispensable element of the efforts to operationalize the agreement in the Summit Outcome document. Their participation in public discussions allows appreciating fully the extensive work of the Commission, including regional consultations and research papers. Their accounts are important when the concept is transferred to situations it was not developed to respond to. At the same time, for their professional and personal involvement in these efforts for a long time, these personalities will not be able to provide leadership for the United Nations to move forward on the operationalization based on the minimum common denominator that could be deducted from the drafting history and final wording of the Outcome Document and ongoing discussions among Member States.

Under Gareth Evan's leadership, the International Crisis Group applied the concept of the responsibility to protect as developed by the ICISS on the situations in Darfur, Uganda and Zimbabwe. The application of the concept on Darfur concentrated mainly on the criteria for the use of non-consensual military intervention.[219] With regard to Northern Uganda, Crisis Group argued that the Security Council could consider the situation as Kampala failed to protect the population from attacks by the Lord's Resistance Army (LRA).[220] With regard to Zimbabwe, Crisis Group considered that operation 'Murambatsvina' in 2005 provided the international community with a clear instance of the responsibility to

218 Ramesh Thakur, in: Conference Report, SEF Symposium 2007, The "Responsibility to Protect: Progress, Empty Promise or a License for "Humanitarian" Intervention?, Bonn, 2008, p. 5f.

219 Getting into Darfur, Crisis Group Africa Briefing No. 43, 12 October 2006, p. 15 et seq.

220 A Strategy for Ending Northern Uganda's Crisis, Crisis Group Africa Briefing No. 35, p. 13 et seq.

protect.[221] Other civil society organizations started to develop case studies of applying the responsibility to protect on past conflicts[222] or current situations. However, the reports did not offer conclusions or recommendations regarding the strategic application of a continuum of civil and military measures that could lead, ultimately, to non-consensual military action.

Since 2002, the World Federalist Movement (WFM) has conducted consultations with civil society organizations from all regions to discuss the ICISS report and its implementation. Following the consultations, in 2003, WFM established a project to engage civil society in the advancement of the responsibility to protect in order to achieve early and effective response by governments and the international community to emerging humanitarian crises. Following the 2005 World Summit, WFM took a new initiative to build a global civil society coalition for the responsibility to protect. In order to facilitate building a global coalition with representatives from organizations from all regions, WFM organized a series of regional roundtables to discuss the implementation of the responsibility to protect. The summaries of these roundtables are a unique source of insight in the political, legal and cultural considerations of civil society in different regions that often contrast the position of their respective governments.[223] Other civil society organizations also reviewed the acceptance of the responsibility to protect in different regions of the world as a basis for advocacy of governments at the level of the United Nations.[224] Careful analysis of these findings can make a valuable contribution to establish the minimum common denominator for the implementation of the agreement in the Summit Outcome.

Oxfam International supported the premise of the responsibility to protect that armed interventions are sometimes a necessary last resort. Different from other humanitarian organization, Oxfam did not have a blanket policy rejecting any military intervention. Thus, Oxfam invoked the responsibility to protect as the rationale for international support for the situation in Somalia[225].

In February 2008, a coalition of concerned civil society organizations launched the Global Center for the responsibility to protect at the City University of New York as an independent research and advocacy body dedicated to effective global responses to genocide, ethnic cleansing, crimes against humanity and war crimes. The Centre was tasked to consolidate international acceptance and ensure the

221 Zimbabwe's Operation Murambatsvina: The Tipping Point? Crisis Group Africa Report No. 97, 17 April 2005, p. 16.

222 See for a review of East Timor, fYROM and Burundi *Human Rights Center*, University of California, Berkeley, The Responsibility to Protect (R2P): Moving the Campaign Forward, 2007, p. 66 et seq.

223 Information on the roundtables is available at http://www.responsibilitytoprotect.org/index.php/pages/1

224 Human Rights Center, University of California, Berkeley, loc. cit., p. 8 et seq.; Development and Peace Foundation, The Responsibility to Protect (R2P): A way forward – or rather part of the problem, Foreign Voices, No. 1, February 2008.

225 Oxfam, International NGOs cannot Adequately Respond to the Unfolding Humanitarian Catastrophe in Somalia, press release, 30 October 2007.

application in practice of the responsibility to protect as adopted at the 2005 World Summit. Secretary-General Ban Ki Moon issued a welcoming statement at the occasion.[226]

The Global Center could make an important contribution to furthering the acceptance of the responsibility to protect through the facilitation of discussions among Member States and civil society and through providing independent expert advice on issues related to its implementation. In this regard, it is important that the Center intends to have a strong North-South character and will be supported by associated centers in Europe, Africa and Latin America. However, with a view to the two former ICISS co-chairs Gareth Evans and Mohamed Sahnoun chairing its International Board, the civil society organizations participating in the initiative[227] and its main donors[228], the Center might be perceived as promoting a particular interpretation of the Summit Outcome document rather than trying to explore common ground for future implementation.

Following the 2005 World Summit, supporters of an operationalization of the agreement on the responsibility to protect organized a series of conferences with a view to agree on joint activities and strategies. These conferences covered national and international advocacy,[229] the normative and political content[230], and made important contributions to the development of any future implementation strategy. However, the majority of events took place in North America or Western Europe and involved the same limited number of active participants and presenters. Notably, the conferences rarely included representatives of Member States and civil society groups that have been perceived as being opposed to making quick progress on implementation.[231] Therefore, the need for an informed and mediated discussion between the different groups outside the context of the General Assembly remains a key priority in order to make progress within the United Nations. There is a need to agree among Member States on the procedure how to arrive at a meaningful discussion in the General Assembly.

Some Member States, officials of the United Nations and civil society organizations tried to benefit from the public attention on the responsibility to

226 Secretary-General's message on the opening of the Global Centre for the Responsibility to Protect, available at http://globalr2p.org/pdf/SGlaunch.pdf

227 The Global Center for the Responsibility to Protect is an initiative of the International Crisis Group, Human Rights Watch, Oxfam International, Refugees International and the Institute for Global Policy.

228 The main donors include Australia, Belgium, Canada, the Netherlands, Norway, Rwanda, the United Kingdom, the John D. and Catherine T. MacArthur Foundation and the Open Society Institute.

229 The Human Rights Center at the University of California, Berkeley, Stopping Mass Atrocities: An International Conference on the Responsibility to Protect, March 2007.

230 The Responsibility to Protect: A Framework for Confronting Identity-based Atrocities, The Benjamin N. Cardozo Law School, March 2008.

231 See for an example for a more inclusive conference The Stanley Foundation (ed.), Actualizing the Responsibility to Protect. 43rd Conference on the United Nations of the Next Decade, Evora (Portugal), June 2008.

protect following the Summit to promote their policies and expand the application to issues previously not discussed in this context. Among others, it was suggested to extend the application of the responsibility to protect to the consequences of climate change, HIV/ AIDS or natural disasters such as in Myanmar. Academic writing concentrated notably on the determination of the responsibility to protect as a legal obligation or emerging international norm.

C. Dressing the naked king - Towards a framework of implementation

1. The possible role for the United Nations in the implementation of the responsibility to protect

1.1 Possible scenario for the application of the responsibility to protect

A review of the possible role of the United Nations in the implementation of the responsibility to protect requires consensus on the basic characteristics of situations, where the agreement in the Summit Outcome would be applicable. Elements for such a scenario can be deducted from the ICISS report, the drafting history of the Summit Outcome document, the limited practice of United Nations organs and bodies and other documents, and statements by United Nations officials, Member States and civil society.

When developing the concept, the ICISS concentrated mainly on the situations in Kosovo, Rwanda, Srebrenica and Somalia in the 1990s.[232] The approach of the responsibility to protect sought to generate a consensus on the most effective response in cases of large-scale killing, ethnic cleansing and crimes against humanity. In order to create this consensus, the responsibility to protect could not be extended across the range of human rights violations and internal conflicts just because they might deteriorate into international crimes in the long-term.[233] After the publication of the report, members of the Commission argued that Iraq was a possible case for the application of the responsibility to protect today and in the late 1980s and early 1990s, but not in 2003. Gareth Evans considered the situations in Burundi and Macedonia excellent examples for how the preventive dimension of the responsibility to protect would have worked, while he cautioned to characterize other cases of human rights violations or conflict in this context.[234] Later he added Darfur, Kenya, Sri Lanka and Zimbabwe as situations, where the responsibility to protect had prima facie application.[235] At another occasion, he added the Holocaust to the list of 'never again' situations which the responsibility to protect sought to address. He illustrated the exceptional character of the situations by arguing that the International Crisis Group identified about 70 different country situations where

232 ICISS Report, FN. 35, p. 1 et seq.
233 Evans, FN. 217.
234 Evans, FN. 213.
235 *Evans*, FN. 52, p. 6.

deadly conflict took place or was about to take place, including violations of human rights and humanitarian law, but only ten to twelve would qualify for the application of the responsibility to protect.[236]

On the basis of the minimum common denominator that appears from the history of the responsibility to protect in the United Nations, its legal content and the institutional practice of principal organs and other bodies to date, it can be concluded that the responsibility to protect would apply to situations that are exceptional for the grave and serious violations of human rights and humanitarian law and where such violations would be either imminent or already ongoing. However, the criteria and indicators for the exceptional character of the situation and the application would remain vague and open to political determinations. Relevant situations would be known already to the international community as at risk of conflict and human rights violations, while Member States might not agree on an exceptional risk, in particular of genocide, war crimes and crimes against humanity. The countless number of governments, international organizations, civil society organizations and individuals collecting data and information from every country in the world on almost any subject do not make it appear likely to expect that genocide, war crimes or crimes against humanity are imminent or taking place already unnoticed. Even a country as closed to the outside world as North Korea became subject to human rights investigations based on satellite imagery and information gathered mainly from deserters and refugees.[237] As the cases from the past suggest, most likely the United Nations will be involved already to some extend through e.g. a country team, a humanitarian presence, technical cooperation projects or the mandates of human rights treaty bodies and special mechanisms of the Human Rights Council. The situation might as well be considered already within the agenda of the Security Council or the General Assembly.

1.2 Existing capacities regarding the responsibility to prevent, react and rebuild

A review of the possible role of the United Nations in the implementation of the agreement in the Summit Outcome document will require a detailed assessment of existing capacities to assist Member States in meeting their individual and collective responsibility to protect. The reports on the involvement of the United Nations in Rwanda and Srebrenica, the Kosovo Report by the Independent International Commission as well as other relevant lessons-learnt exercises provide valuable material to identify the specific demands on the United Nations in situations of imminent or ongoing mass atrocities. The assessment should include previous

236 Evans, FN. 212.

237 See *David Hawk/ U.S. Committee for Human Rights in North Korea*, The Hidden Gulag. Exposing North Korea's Prison Camps (2003); Failure to Protect: A Call for the UN Security Council to Act on North Korea, Report commissioned by Vaclav Havel, Kjell Magne Bondevik, Elie Wiesel (2006).

reviews of concepts related to the responsibility to prevent, to react and to rebuild, such as prevention of armed conflict, prevention of genocide and protection of civilians in armed conflict.[238] The following overview will remain limited in scope and aims at providing suggestions for a future comprehensive review that should involve all United Nations departments, agencies and funds, and include civil society.[239]

At the outset, it is necessary to clarify for the assessment the definition of relevant expressions that lack consistent application in the different reports and public statements.[240] United Nations 'peace operations' undertake conflict prevention, intervention, peacemaking, peacekeeping and peace building. 'Intervention' refers to robust military action aimed at protecting civilians, secure humanitarian access and provide for basic agreement between the parties, e.g. on a cease-fire or humanitarian access. 'Peacemaking' addresses conflict in progress attempting to bring them to a halt, using mainly diplomacy and mediation. Today, 'peacekeeping' provides for a complex model of military and civilian activities to build peace after a civil war. Since the 1990s, peacekeeping operations have been deployed to create rather than secure post conflict situations by trying to divert the different personal, political and external agendas permanently from the military to the political arena.[241] 'Peace building' defines activities addressing the root causes of conflict and establishing the foundation of comprehensive and sustainable peace.

The protection of people from imminent or ongoing genocide, war crimes and crimes against humanity does not require a specific responsibility to protect mandate. Instead, as has been shown in past and present situations, almost any United Nations presence, including the United Nations Country Team (UNCT), humanitarian organizations, cease-fire monitoring missions or election monitors, can contribute to increase the level of protection based on their existing mandates. To this end, the assessment of capacities should result in the development of a tool box of available measures for the United Nations departments, agencies and funds.

238 See e.g. An Agenda for Peace. U.N.-Doc. A/47/277 - S/24111 of 17 June 1992; Supplement to the Agenda for Peace, U.N.-Doc. A/50/60 - S/1995/1 of 3 January 1995; The causes of conflict and the promotion of durable peace and sustainable development in Africa. Report of the Secretary-General, U.N.-Doc. S/1998/318 of 13 April 1998; Interim Report of the Secretary-General on the prevention of armed conflict, U.N.-Doc. A/58/365-S/2003/888 of 12 September 2008.

239 *Evans*, FN. 52, p. 79 et seq. reviews existing measures of early-warning, prevention, intervention and post-conflict peace building, however, without establishing the specific contribution they could make to the responsibility to protect versus crisis and conflict in general.

240 The following definitions follow the Report of the Panel on United Nations Peace Operations, U.N.-Doc. A/55/305 – S/2000/809 of 21 August 2000, para. 10 et seq., with some modifications.

241 Op. cit., p. 21

1.2.1 Existing capacities regarding the responsibility to prevent

Following the basic characteristics of the scenario to which the responsibility to protect would apply, the responsibility to prevent would be limited to causes related to the occurrence of the particular crimes mentioned in the Summit Outcome document, in the short to medium-term, depending on the predictability of future developments of an exceptional character. In order to avoid applying the responsibility to prevent to situations of conflict and human rights violations across the board, an agreed set of indicators for the assessment of country situations as exceptional would be required. Finally, the United Nations require capacities to assist Member States in the implementation of their responsibility to prevent.

1.2.1.1 Early-warning capacities

Early-warning is universally accepted to be one of the pillars of effective prevention.[242] Various United Nations departments, funds and agencies, and civil society established methodologies and capacities to collect and analyze early-warning information according to their respective requirements.[243] In addition, there are currently 34 distinct, active mandates from the General Assembly, the Security Council and the Economic and Social Council related to early warning.[244] The multiplicity of initiatives and mandates reflects the difficulty the United Nations has experienced in finding a consensus how to fulfill this function most effectively. In 1987, for example, the Office for Research and the Collection of Information was created for 'analysis and monitoring of potential threats to international peace and

242 See for an overview *Frederick Barton/ Karen von Hippel*, Early Warning? A Review of Conflict Prediction Models and Systems, PCR Special Project Briefing, Center for Strategic and International Studies, February 2008.

243 Capacities include the Executive Committee Peace and Security, the Executive Committee on Humanitarian Affairs, the Interagency Framework Team on Prevention, the Inter Agency Standing Committee (sub-working group on Preparedness and Contingency Planning), DPA (Peace-building support offices, Special Representatives and Envoys of the SG, Resource group on conflict prevention), DPKO (Peace-keeping operations), DDA (Standardized instrument for reporting military expenditure, Register of conventional arms, UN Disarmament Yearbook, DDA Quarterly Updates, reports, publications, papers), OCHA (Humanitarian Early Warning System), DESA (Task force on conflict prevention, Peacebuilding Portal), OHCHR (Field Presences, Human rights components of DPA/ DPKO missions, CERD and CCPR early-warning procedures, urgent appeals procedure of Special Rapporteurs, 1503 Procedure), UNHCR (Field Presences, early-warning system), UNDP (Bureau for Crisis Prevention and Recovery, Peace and development advisors in UN Country Teams, Conflict Analysis Development Initiative), World Bank (Conflict Prevention and Reconstruction Unit).

244 Mandating and Delivering: Analysis and Recommendations to Facilitate the Review of Mandates, U.N.-Doc. A/60/733 of 30 March 2006.

security'[245] and early warning, but was disbanded after just a few years due to resistance from Member States resulting in inadequate resources.[246] The Brahimi report recommended creating an Information and Strategic Analysis Secretariat of the ECPS in order for the key departments to cooperate more closely within a strategic approach of the United Nations to conflict prevention, peace-keeping and peace building.[247]

Meanwhile, there have been important signs of international political commitment to improve genocide early warning. In July 2004, the Secretary-General appointed a Special Adviser on the Prevention of Genocide with an explicit mandate to

> act as a mechanism of early warning to the Secretary-General, and through him to the Security Council, by bringing to their attention potential situations that could result in genocide.[248]

At the 2005 World Summit, Heads of State and Government declared that '[t]he international community should [...] support the United Nations in establishing an early warning capability' in connection with the pronouncement the responsibility to protect. The initial work of the Special Adviser related to genocide early-warning provides a good starting point for the review of United Nations capacities in this regard.[249] In addition, external models related to the conditioning of people involved in the violations against civilians[250] and the eight stages of genocide[251] provide examples for the analysis of existing information.

Specific methodology relevant for the early-warning of genocide, war crimes and crimes against humanity is readily available and includes genocide indicators adopted by the Committee on the Elimination of Racial Discrimination (CERD)[252],

245 *Bertrand G. Ramcharan*, Early-Warning at the United Nations: the First Experiment. International Journal of Refugee Law, Vol. 1, 1989, p. 379 et seq.

246 *Walter Dorn*, Intelligence at UN Headquarters? Intelligence and National Security, Vol. 20, 2005, p. 440 et seq. See also *Thant Myint-U/ Sofia Busch*, Knowledge Needs at the UN Secretariat in the Field of Peace and Security: Reflections from 'The Knowledge Project' 2004.

247 Brahimi report, FN. 240, para. 65 et seq.

248 Letter dated 12 July 2004 from the Secretary-General addressed to the President of the Security Council, U.N.-Doc. S/2004/567 of 13 July 2004.

249 Report of the Secretary-General on the implementation of the Five Point Action Plan and the activities of the Special Adviser on the Prevention of Genocide, U.N.-Doc. E/CN.4/2006/84 of 1 February 2006.

250 *Hugo Slim/ Deborah Mancini-Griffoli*, Interpreting Violence. Anti-Civilian Thinking and Practice and How to Argue Against It More Effectively, Center for Humanitarian Dialogue, Geneva, 2007, p. 19 et seq.

251 Developed by Gregory Stanton. See http://www.genocidewatch.org/8stages.htm

252 Declaration on the prevention of genocide, U.N.-Doc. CERD/C/66/1 of 17 October 2005; Decision on follow-up to the declaration on the prevention of genocide: indicators of patterns of systematic and massive racial discrimination, U.N.-Doc. CERD/C/67/1 of 14 October 2005.

genocide risk assessment and early warning models developed by academia[253], the European Commission's check list for root causes of conflict indicators[254], and the Global Risk Matrix of the Office for the Coordination of Humanitarian Affairs. These methodologies are useful to identify and analyze situations, where vulnerable groups are at risk, but they have limitations for the development of policy action to prevent or halt in particular genocide, war crimes and crimes against humanity. For instance, experience indicates that the warning signs of genocide may differ significantly from those of even closely related phenomena like civil war and state failure. CERD indicators, while specifically designed to anticipate genocide through racial discrimination in national law and practice, are of little help in devising short- to medium-term policies within a continuum of steps as required by the responsibility to protect. Other human rights treaty-bodies and special mechanisms established by the Human Rights Council receive and analyze relevant information on a daily basis. However, so far OHCHR did not develop any systematic early-warning system for human rights emergencies even though, according to its own account, its mandate includes the prevention of human rights violations.[255]

A more general problem related to early warning is the limited extent to which information is used by policymakers even when high quality information appears to exist. While United Nations departments, agencies and funds have invested heavily in improving the methods for producing accurate warnings, substantially less attention has been paid to overcome difficulties in fostering the use of early-warning information in a policy context. In the case of Rwanda and Srebrenica, basic information on the facts on the ground was available to Member States, but they lacked analysis of the data and its translation into policy prescriptions, as well as the will to act.[256] Furthermore, looking at the situations in the past that could have been considered under the responsibility to protect, none came as a surprise. Most cases of massive violations of human rights have been well expected and announced.[257]

In this regard, United Nations practice is often naïve and limited, as it concentrates on documenting the facts of events. All early-warning systems for genocide have identified the same 10-15 situations at risk.[258] The challenge remains how to bring the information to the attention of Member States, in particular in the

253 See e.g. *Barbara Harff*, No Lessons Learned from the Holocaust? Assessing Risks of Genocide and Political Mass Murder since 1955, American Political Science Review, Vol. 97, 2003, p. 57 et seq.

254 See e.g. International Crisis Group, EU Crisis Response Capabilities Revisited, Europe Report Nr.160 of 17 January 2005.

255 See for the mandate of the High-Commissioner U.N.-Doc. A/RES/41/141 of 20 December 1993 and http://www.ohchr.org/EN/AboutUs/Pages/Mandate.aspx

256 ICISS report, FN. 35, p. 70 et seq.

257 See *David Hamburg*, Preventing Genocide: Practical Steps Toward Early Detection and Effective Action, Paradigm Publishers, 2008.

258 See e.g. *Harff*, FN. 253; Stanton, FN. 251; *Lawrence Woocher*, Early Warning for the Prevention of Genocide and Mass Atrocities, Paper presented at the annual meeting of the International Studies Association 48th Annual Convention, Chicago,28 February 2007.

Security Council,[259] and create political will to act or, more precisely, propose targeted measures within an overall strategy to generate political pressure, at home and abroad, on Member States to act. For the motivation of political actors to implement their responsibility to protect, a different kind of information will be required. Rather than establishing the facts, more time and resources should be spent on the analysis of high-risk situations to identify alleged perpetrators, command structures, international links, political interests of main actors, weaknesses and personal involvement. In fact, this approach would create a completely different information gathering and early-warning system from those currently available to the United Nations. This information would allow the Secretariat to propose effective measures short of intervention to the Security Council. In addition, the process of gathering information should aim at generating a consensus within the Secretariat on the exceptional character of a situation as a prerequisite for the development of a joint strategy and the steps for its implementation.

1.2.1.2 Early-action capacities

When defining the responsibility to prevent, the ICISS distinguished in the prevention of root causes for conflict and direct prevention efforts. The Commission referred to the widespread recognition that armed conflicts could not be understood without reference to such root causes as poverty, political repression and uneven distribution of resources.[260] Thus, root cause prevention has many dimensions and may mean to address political needs, economic deprivation, legal protection and sectoral reform within the State security services. Direct prevention may address the same areas, but with different instruments, reflecting the shorter time available.[261] In the Summit Outcome document, the responsibility to prevent is not explained further, but rather expressed like an appeal.

The informal Working Group established by the Executive Committee for Peace and Security to develop a repertoire of measures to assist Member States in their responsibility to protect identified a range of possibilities which the international community could consider to protect, in general, vulnerable civilians in conflict situations. However, as explained above, the Working Group encountered difficulties in identifying measures particularly suited to the prevention of genocide, war crimes, ethnic cleansing and crimes against humanity. The Working Group identified different diplomatic, humanitarian and other measures, including high-level fact-finding resulting in a public or private report and briefing to the Security Council with recommendations, discreet fact-finding that could lead to internal reporting and contribute to the formulation of policy, early deployment of

259 Report of the Independent Inquiry into the actions of the United Nations during the 1994 genocide in Rwanda, U.N.-Doc. S/1999/1257 of 16 December 1999, p. 33.

260 See for details on root cause prevention efforts ICISS report, FN. 25, p. 22 et seq.

261 See for details on direct prevention efforts, op. cit., p. 23 et seq.

assessment teams with a mandate framed by the legal obligations related to the particular crimes, discreet or public approaches to a State by the Secretariat to draw attention to a situation and expose shortcomings in protection, communication through a statement by a high level official or other means of advocacy, capacity-building through the provision of expert advice and technical assistance to relevant State institutions and steps to ensure physical protection of civilians in refugee camps through a humanitarian, human rights or police presence. The imposition of sanctions by the Security Council could play an important role in support of preventive diplomacy by providing leverage to bring parties to the bargaining table, to encourage actors to take steps set out by the international community to mitigate threats, or to discourage actors from continuing activities that are deemed threats to international peace and security.

So far, this list is mixing institutions, means, general strategies and specific measures and would require a more systematic review. Nevertheless, this list could be developed further through a systematic assessment.

It has been suggested that the Human Rights Council could be mandated within the United Nations to implement the responsibility to prevent.[262] Pursuant to paragraph 10 of General Assembly resolution 60/251 of 15 March 2006, the Human Rights Council can hold special sessions at the request of a member of the Council with the support of one third of its membership. So far, the Council held seven special sessions related to the human rights situations in the Occupied Palestinian Territory, Lebanon, Darfur, Myanmar as well as on the global food crisis and, twice, on Israeli military incursions on the Occupied Palestinian Territory. The special sessions resulted in resolutions by the Council condemning violations by the government, some deciding to set up fact-finding mechanisms.[263] However, in those resolutions the Human Rights Council did not propose a continuum of steps to prevent future violations, including indicators and timelines. Ultimately, the implementation of the responsibility to prevent will require clarification of the relationship with the Security Council, which remains unclear as long as many Member States argue that, as part of the General Assembly, the Human Rights Council mandates should be strictly separated.

The Expert Group on Darfur appointed by the Human Rights Council provided an initial experience for a general strategy of cooperation with governments on specific measures to halt or prevent large-scale violations of human rights and humanitarian law. The reports on Kosovo, Rwanda, Somalia and Srebrenica would provide additional examples that could help defining sets of generic measures for the prevention of genocide, war crimes and crimes against humanity. Ultimately, country-specific measures will have to be developed on a case-by-case basis

262 Arbour, FN. 101.

263 U.N.-Doc. A/HRC/S-1/3 of 18 July 2006; U.N.-Doc. A/HRC/S-2/2 of 17 August 2006; U.N.-Doc. A/HRC/S-3/2 of 20 November 2006; U.N.-Doc. A/HRC/S-4/5 of 22 January 2007; U.N.-Doc. A/HRC/S-5/2 of 28 November 2007; U.N.-Doc. A/HRC/S-6/2 of 31 March 2008; U.N.-Doc. A/HRC/S-7/2 of 17 July 2008.

according to a common analysis of the situation on the ground and an effective early-warning system to provide the information required by the different decision making bodies, including the Secretariat, United Nations agencies and funds, the Security Council and other organs and mechanisms.

1.2.2 Existing capacities regarding the responsibility to react

According to the Summit Outcome document, the responsibility to react should include diplomatic, humanitarian and other measures under Chapter VI, VII and VIII of the Charter. Thus, it can be assumed that the primary responsibility would be vested in the Security Council. Article 33, paragraph 1 of the Charter provides for a list of generic measures that the Council could employ in order to carry out its mandate, including negotiation, enquiry, mediation, conciliation, arbitration, judicial settlement and resort to regional agencies.

In previous cases of gross and serious violations of human rights and humanitarian law, the Security Council or other United Nations organs took steps e.g. to provide humanitarian aid to refugees and internally displaced persons, undertake a demarche with the government concerned, condemn the events in an official statement or resolution, appoint a Special Representative as interlocutor for the government, appoint a commission of inquiry or fact-finding mission, refer the situation to the International Criminal Court, establish an international or mixed international tribunal, mandate an international civilian and military presence, initiate targeted sanctions against individuals allegedly responsible for the violations, initiate an arms embargo and other measures to limit the resources of the government or initiate a special session of the Human Rights Council. In addition, most of the measures mentioned above in the context of the responsibility to prevent would be applicable as well.

While all of these measures can provide effective support to Member States and the international community to meet their individual and collective responsibility to react, a review of the practice of the United Nations in addressing the situations in Darfur, Rwanda, Somalia or Srebrenica has documented that these measures are employed separately, consecutively or in parallel, most often, however, without a recognizable strategy regarding a continuum of consensual and non-consensual steps. Normally, these decisions lack indicators and benchmarks to review their effectiveness. It is evident that often the decision about the application of these measures is taken in lieu of a consensus on the involvement of the United Nations and a strategy, how to address the situation most effectively.

In addition, while these measures are perceived to be taken on behalf of the United Nations, the respective organs and bodies often approach their mandates in isolation from the work of others, directly relevant for their own. In the case of Darfur and Somalia, Member States insisted during informal consultations in the Security Council to delete references in draft resolutions to the respective resolutions of the Human Rights Council and included only general references to the human rights situation.

1.2.2.1 Civilian capacities

A comprehensive review of available civilian capacities regarding the responsibility to react is well beyond the framework of this book. Instead, the assessment will be limited to those measures that have been identified already within the discussion on the operationalization of the responsibility to protect as supporting Member States in meeting their responsibility to react, short of military or police measures.

Following the ICISS report, the High-level panel proposed the deployment, inter alia, of human rights and humanitarian missions in order to assist the cessation of violence through mediation and other tools and the protection of people through their presence.[264] The ECPS Working Group listed the deployment of human rights monitors among the means to prevent or halt large-scale violence against vulnerable populations. Increased fact-finding missions initiated by the Secretary-General as a measure of prevention and reaction has been proposed earlier.[265] However, the effectiveness of fact-finding missions will always depend on the possibility to introduce their findings and recommendations into policy discussions in the General Assembly or the Security Council, including respective initiatives by the Secretary-General.

At conferences on the responsibility to protect, participants quickly agree on the importance to develop further the capacity of Member States and the United Nations to meet their responsibility to prevent and responsibility to rebuild. This approach risks moving away the important focus that the responsibility to protect provides for the development of civilian capacities within the United Nations to respond to ongoing or imminent large-scale violence.

According to the most likely scenario for the application of the responsibility to react, the United Nations could respond to ongoing or imminent large-scale violence initially within existing capacities and mandates following a common strategic approach based on a common understanding of the causes and pattern of violence in the situation at hand. Some elements for a common strategic approach will be suggested below.

The implementation of the responsibility to react, which can include non-consensual military means as a last resort, will constitute a particular challenge for humanitarian organizations. In the most likely scenario, humanitarian organizations will be on the ground already and seek to sustain access to vulnerable groups and uphold the humanitarian principles of humanity, neutrality, impartiality and independence. In particular with a view to the principle of neutrality, the responsibility to protect must not be considered to cover all areas of humanitarian

264 High-level Panel report, FN. 40, para. 201.
265 Brahimi report, FN. 240, p. ix

protection in all emergencies. Instead, the concept is limited to exceptional situations which define the application of the principle of neutrality by the United Nations system: When genocide, war crimes and crimes against humanity take place on a scale comparable to the situation in Rwanda or Srebrenica, humanitarian assistance cannot continue business usual. While humanitarian access might initially be limited, activities implementing the responsibility to react aim at the physical protection of vulnerable groups and the creation of some space to ensure their survival. Thus, such activities cannot be perceived as undermining humanitarian principles.[266] Protection and access cannot be the sole priority as long as United Nations limited activities only keep the victims alive in camps over years and, thereby, contribute to the intent of the government.[267] In many cases of mass atrocities, Member States justified their limitations to act with the need to deliver humanitarian aid and upholding humanitarian principles. At the same time, humanitarian activities often serve as a powerful justification for regular access to threatened populations. Humanitarian needs assessments offer key opportunities for international visibility in areas of imminent violence. The provision of international aid can be a crucial door opener for an international presence in the first place. Therefore, joint United Nations strategies in situations, where genocide, war crimes or crimes against humanity might occur, require general guidelines for the cooperation between humanitarian, political and other United Nations actors as well as a particular road map for the case at hand. Crucial time will be lost, if the interpretation of principles and their limitations towards cooperation are discussed every time a joint United Nations strategy is required. Furthermore, perpetrators are very skillful in playing out divisions between United Nations departments, agencies and funds.

Many different strategies and approaches to the protection of civilians have been developed. They have to be reviewed for their applicability to imminent or ongoing genocide, war crimes and crimes against humanity, however, outside the political context of the protection of civilians' discussion within the Security Council. Any review of capacities to implement the responsibility to react should look at the three main approaches to protect civilians, i.e. deterrence of potential perpetrators, support to civilians to protect themselves, and influence reformers and others to change attitudes.[268]

Ultimately, the protection of vulnerable groups from international crimes is the responsibility of their State of residence. Any United Nations action in situations of

266 Incorporating a conflict sensitive approach into humanitarian planning and programming propose *Maria Lange/ Mick Quinn*, Meeting the Challenges, International Alert, December 2003; elements of an operational framework for the contribution of humanitarian organizations to the fight against impunity *Anne-Marie La Rosa*, Humanitarian organizations and international criminal tribunals, or trying to square the circle, International Review of the Red Cross, Vol. 88, 2006, p. 169 et seq.

267 See Press Release SC/9178.

268 *Liam Mahoney*, Proactive Presence. Field Strategies for civilian protection, Centre for Humanitarian Dialogue, 2006.

imminent or ongoing violence should seek to complement and strengthen the activities of national institutions and civil society organizations. Violence is often preceded by a breakdown of relationship between the government, its people and among different groups within society. While a long-term change of the underlying root-causes would require long-term strategies and compromise, large scale violence prevents targeted groups and individuals from demanding government attention. Genocide, war crimes and crimes against humanity are often committed in a context of stigmatization of ethnic or other groups, attacks on IDPs perceived as supporting the adversaries, and persecution of civil society. United Nations activities should take into account their positive contribution to changing perceptions and attitudes by interacting with stigmatized groups and individuals and actively setting counter-examples for diversity and tolerance. The United Nations will have to make choices as to the degree of encouragement they can give to civil society actors and individuals to take risks. While the targeted population will make its own choices and might consider risk-taking as part of the process to solve the situation, the United Nations should enable national and local actors to make conscious decisions, including a clear understanding of the limits of the United Nations, rather than trying to decide on the acceptable risk-level on behalf of the vulnerable groups.

The United Nations at country and headquarter level should establish daily contacts with key political actors at the national and local level of the state concerned. Confidential dialogue remains an important tool for these contacts even in times of public pressure on the United Nations. Even in situation where the State is the main perpetrator of violence, approaching simultaneously the national and local level of the military, police, judiciary or government agency that can improve the protection of vulnerable groups, change the dynamics of the conflict. In this regard, it would be important to add qualified personnel, including high-ranking military and police personnel to the United Nations presence on the ground.[269]

In situations of imminent or ongoing large-scale violence, the United Nations should use any possibility to convene and bridge between parties. Even though no solution to the problems might be found, communication and dialogue can have a positive impact on the situation. Often, the stakes might be too high for an agreement on future peace negotiations or a cease-fire and concentration on these issues might overlook 'low hanging fruit' opportunities. In addition, participants in those contacts often benefit from increased protection. Short of direct contacts, shuttle diplomacy should be considered.

A particular challenge for any United Nations activities will be the establishment of a dialogue with possible perpetrators of grave human rights violations. In this regard, the limits and complementarities of different measures have to be taken into account. In the situations at hand, the United Nations has to establish contacts with all actors, who control territory and people and have the capacity to harm civilians. The involvement of the International Criminal Court or another investigative body could serve as a support as well as an obstacle to the establishment of such contacts.

269 See for more details *Mahoney*, op. cit., p. 49 et seq.

Some perpetrators might seek to interrupt all contacts with the United Nations out of fear of being arrested and transferred to The Hague; others might be encouraged to exculpate themselves. At the same time, such an involvement could lead to internal friction and difficulties for the government to continue its policy. However, these influences must be part of a careful analysis of the conflict. Notwithstanding these difficulties, it will be important for the United Nations to make personal accountability clear to perpetrators during the events.[270]

A United Nations presence at locations throughout the country can serve as a constant deterrent to potential abusers and build confidence of the population. The expansion of tasks and activities has to be tailored to the size of the presence. In order to uphold any impact in situations of imminent violence, the United Nations must be ready and willing to respond to urgent calls, go to dangerous places and intervene quickly. In this regard, security phases cannot apply unless the United Nations would exclude from the outset that it could play a non-military role in such situations. The presence in a conflict zone must be coordinated between different agencies to maximize the impact of a very limited number of staff.

Targeted public reports on certain pattern of human rights violations can support initiatives towards a dialogue and encourage parties to participate. In this regard, reporting mechanisms often lack a strategy on follow-up to the results, the target audience and recommendations that might be most powerful taking into account other initiatives. Within the context of the responsibility to protect, public human rights reports should include indicators, deadlines and follow up opportunities for the international community to assess, at a certain stage, whether the government concerned 'manifestly failed' to implement important steps within the continuum.

Accompanying threatened people, including by staying with them in IDP camps and villages, is physically risky but has saved lives in various occasions.[271] In situations of imminent or ongoing violence, it requires careful security analysis as well as a clear signal to perpetrators that any violence against the presence, including e.g. kidnapping or cutting off communications or food, will have direct consequences. Thus, such activities in a conflict zone are difficult to imagine without a military capacity for immediate response.

The presence of senior United Nations officers, Special Rapporteurs or representatives of Member States can send an important signal to perpetrators, if used strategically to cover as many threatened locations as possible. In 2004, a chain of foreign ministers, United Nations officials and others visited Darfur relying on the operational support of the United Nations Mission in Sudan (UNMIS). However, their presence was concentrated on the same limited number of camps and villages and remote areas remained uncovered. While security and scheduling challenges for VIP missions are evident, their presence risks to send a soothing signal to the perpetrators and the victims that, in fact, the government is in control of the

270 Rwanda report, FN. 259, p. 39.

271 *Mahoney*, FN. 268, p. 69

international community. Priority should be given to locations where such visits could have the greatest impact on the protection of vulnerable groups.

Situations of imminent or ongoing violence require a public diplomacy strategy on complementary messages of the different United Nations actors involved. The objective of the strategy should be a concrete improvement of the situation rather than creating headlines. Often, statements by high-ranking United Nations officials in such situations are motivated more by the concern to be on the record and respond to public pressure than by a supporting and joint United Nations strategy. In most of the situations in the past, there has been a lack of international interest in taking robust steps to protect vulnerable groups, if necessary, through an effective United Nations presence. In most situations of large-scale violence, the Secretariat will face the challenge of persuading Member States and the international community to step up their efforts. Pessimism about the lack of political will and strong perceptions of the interests of Security Council members have been prevalent within the Secretariat and often lead to hesitation and self-censoring.[272]

The main requirement of a public diplomacy strategy is agreement on the objective and coherent messages responding to carefully analyzed perceptions of Member States. One argument often stated against public messages is the risk of losing access, if the United Nations is too outspoken about protection issues. However, the specific risk in a given situation must be carefully analyzed and a statement linked to concrete demands on the practical level might be more effective than general denunciation. In situations of imminent or ongoing violence, governments are vulnerable with regard to their international reputation and the loss of political benefit and relationships in economic and other areas. This effect might as well include their international partners. In general, a correlation between statements and harassment on the ground is not statistically clear. The risk of shutting down channels of dialogue with accused abusers remains powerful for all public statements.[273]

A possible overall strategy to maintain impartiality and be perceived as such by the parties would be for the United Nations to refer to one of the main characteristics of the responsibility to protect and act as advocate of the vulnerable population. Reflecting the views of the victims and limiting arguments to physical protection might take away many of the stereotypes and allegations involved in this kind of crimes. Recalling the moral and legal dimension of genocide, war crimes and crimes against humanity might also encourage a dialogue between parties. Showing appreciation and interest in moderate leaders could influence positively the dynamics within and between the parties. Neutral space for discussion, targeted workshops and trainings for the military and the police on relevant legal standards might have a positive impact and result in the formation of commissions and other

272 Brahimi report, FN. 240, p. x.

273 A related, but distinct question is the jamming of frequences used by national radio stations to incite violence. See *Jamie Metzl*, Rwandan Genocide and the International Law of Radio Jamming, AJIL, Vol. 91, 1997, p. 628 et seq.

structures. Negotiations on 'humanitarian accords' holding parties accountable for commitments about protection and access could be a good entry point.

At the same time, the Holocaust and, more recently, the refugee crisis following the genocide in Rwanda, made clear that the implementation of the responsibility to react must not be limited by the borders of the State, where the violations take place. Asylum would often be the most immediate and practical assistance to victims of genocide, war crimes and crimes against humanity. Therefore, the international system of refugee protection requires a critical assessment of its possible contribution to the saving of people from such situations.[274]

With regard to the availability of resources, the earlier proposal of a roster of civilian personnel should be revisited in the light of requirements of the implementation of the responsibility to protect.[275] The reserve should include individuals with particular experience and expertise in situations of ongoing large-scale violence.

While a careful review of the practice of the application of the measures that have been employed so far would be required in order to identify or adjust those considered most effective in situations of imminent or ongoing violence, experience has shown that the lack of effective sanctions in case of non-cooperation of States with these mechanisms has been the core deficit of their effective implementation.[276] Research has shown that for any protective activity to be effective a targeted political response to violators is required.[277] While the sanctions system will always be applied to only a limited number of alleged perpetrators based on political considerations of Security Council members, the development of a military option within a joint strategy on a continuum of steps could be applied as a deterrent. While it would not address the root causes, even limited activity for the physical protection of vulnerable groups at risk would change immediately the dynamics of the conflict. It is important to recall in this context that genocide, war crimes and crimes against humanity can hardly be committed without, at least, the indifference of the respective government.

1.2.2.2 Military and police capacities

When reviewing the experience of United Nations action to prevent or halt genocide, war crimes or crimes against humanity in order to establish existing military and police capacities it is important to build a consensus on the definition of

274 See e.g. *Ninette Kelly*, International Refugee Protection Challenges and Opportunities, International Journal of Refugee Law, Vol. 19, No. 3, 2007, p. 401 et seq.

275 Brahimi report, FN. 240, p. xii

276 On the effectiveness of sanctions in general see *Peter Wallensteen/ Carina Staibano/ Mikael Eriksson* (eds.), Making Targeted Sanctions Effective: Guidelines for the Implementation of UN Policy Options, Uppsala University, 2003.

277 *Mahoney*, FN. 268, p. 32

success and failure in these circumstances. The absence of universally applicable measure of success for rating peace operations have led to conflicting conclusions by experts and Member States. The responsibility to react has to be considered as part of a continuum of steps towards Member States meeting fully their responsibility to protect. Within the exceptional circumstances considered in the context of the responsibility to protect, an intervention, even if it fails to produce a timely or complete resolution of the conflict, is preferable to unabated violence.[278] Within the continuum of steps, peacekeeping operations and other existing arrangements involving military acting under the United Nations authority could make valuable contributions to assisting Member States in fulfilling their responsibility to protect. However, the main contribution of the responsibility to protect to solving the dilemma of the principle of non-intervention in internal affairs versus the protection of people from gross human rights violations is the introduction of military intervention by the United Nations as a practical political option. Consequently, rather than reviewing all possible military action for its possible contribution to the responsibility to protect, it will be necessary to concentrate on the experience in intervening in cases of ongoing or imminent genocide, war crimes and crimes against humanity.

Following the experience in Rwanda and Srebrenica, United Nations troops and police who witness violence against civilians should be presumed to be authorized to stop it within their means, in support of basic principles of the United Nations.[279] The basis for action by United Nations peacekeepers to intervene in ongoing or imminent genocide, war crimes and crimes against humanity will often be the mandate of the respective mission to protect the civilian population. Increasingly, the mandate of peacekeeping operations has included similar provisions for the protection of civilians.[280] Ultimately, the key functions identified for the protection of civilians by a civilian presence, i.e. deterrence, encouragement and influence, should as well be applied by any military presence.

Rules of engagement for armed military contingents in each peacekeeping operation are issued by headquarters in New York and derive from the mandate authorized by the Security Council. These rules provide the parameters within which armed military personnel may use different levels of force. They ensure that the use of force by United Nations military personnel is undertaken in accordance with the Charter, the Security Council mandate and the relevant principles of international law, including the laws of armed conflict. Ultimately, generic activities related to the implementation of the responsibility to react have to be reflected in the rules of

278 *Joshua G. Smith*, The Responsibility to Reflect: Learning Lessons from Past Humanitarian Military Interventions, Georgetown University, 2004.

279 Brahimi report, FN. 240, para. 62.

280 According to these provisions, based on Chapter VII of the Charter, the United Nations mission is 'authorized to take the necessary action, in the areas of deployment of its forces and as it deems within its capabilities', see e.g. U.N.-Doc. S/RES/1769 (2007) of 31 July 2007, para. 15.

engagement in order to make best use of available resources and identify gaps and weaknesses.

However, the implementation of the responsibility to react is distinct from the wars between States which national armies primarily prepare, or peacekeeping duties, where troops support delivering supplies, monitoring cease-fire agreements or protecting new governments. Soldiers will be requested to provide physical protection for vulnerable groups from large-scale violence. Often, the international crimes relevant for the responsibility to protect are committed in the context of intrastate conflicts involving armed groups, sometimes established along ethnic lines and with children among their ranks. In addition to the direct impact of violent conflict, civilians are exposed to indirect threats in their attempt to flee to safety, including exposure to sexual violence, disease, lack of access to adequate food, shelter, clean water or healthcare, which could constitute a means of committing such crimes through attrition. These challenges lead to the question on the contribution that troops acting on behalf of the United Nations could make to the implementation of the responsibility to react.

The availability of armed forces, assistance and facilities to the United Nations as provided for in article 43 of the Charter was considered one of the cornerstones of the new, centralized system of collective security.[281] However, since its foundation, the United Nations has struggled to obtain reliable, readily available and rapidly deployable military resources for securing and restoring international peace and security. During the Cold War period, Member States were unwilling to commit their national troops to a supranational mechanism. At the same time, proposals ranging from a permanent United Nations force to a loosely arranged stand-by system have been discussed. In his 1992 Agenda for Peace, Secretary-General Boutros Boutros-Ghali recommended that the Security Council initiate negotiations in accordance with article 43 of the Charter.[282] This initiative led to significant developments with regard to peacekeeping arrangements.

In 1993, the Department of Peacekeeping Operations (DPKO) established the Enhanced UN Standby Arrangement for Military and Civilian Police Capabilities (UNSAS) in the interest of a smooth establishment of peacekeeping operations in times of crisis. The system provides for a simplified uniform procedure for the deployment of forces by Member States and, in April 2005, included 83 Member States.

In 1996, following the failure of United Nations peacekeeping in Bosnia, Rwanda and Somalia, seven Member States, including Austria, Canada, Denmark, the Netherlands, Norway Poland and Sweden, established the Multinational Standby High Readiness Brigade for United Nations Operations (SHIRBRIG) with the aim of providing the United Nations with a rapidly deployable peacekeeping force. Since its inception, 16 additional Member States joined the agreement and SHIRBRIG

281 Frowein/ Krisch, Art. 43, in: *Simma*, FN. 97, para. 1.
282 U.N.-Doc. A/47/227-S/24111 of 17 June 1992, para. 43.

participated in five peacekeeping missions and undertook military capacity building initiatives in Africa.[283]

SHIRBRIG is a multinational brigade dedicated to the rapid temporary deployment of up to 5,000 troops for United Nations peacekeeping operations under Chapter VI and, more recently, Chapter VII of the Charter, subject to prior national approval. The troops are self-sustainable for up to 60 days and should be deployed for no longer than six month; it is expected that the brigade is succeeded by regular, long-term United Nations peacekeepers.

While the different national troop units of the brigade are on-call in their respective country, SHIRBRIG provides for a standing headquarters. The deployment of the brigade under Chapter VII of the Charter is subject to a case-by-case analysis. Potential missions could include more robust interventions. In any case, SHIRBRIG must have the inherent capacity of extended self-defense and to extradite its elements from untenable situations. However, experience has shown that the deployment of the full brigade has become the exception as Member States are reluctant to provide the earmarked troops as pledged. Rather, SHIRBRIG provided key personnel to form the nucleus of a United Nations force headquarters on an interim basis. Furthermore, the delay of national approval mechanisms led to delays in the deployment.

SHIRBRIG operates at low costs, as Denmark provides for the permanent headquarters and the United Nations pays all expenses from the time of deployment, according to UN rules and regulations. The brigade is considered the most advanced multinational mechanism for United Nations peace operations developed to date.

However, the current arrangements are of limited use for the rapid deployment of United Nations forces in response to ongoing or imminent genocide, war crimes and crimes against humanity. First, the stand-by arrangements cannot provide capacities for robust action required in such situations. SHIRBRIG mainly concentrates its activities on planning support and capacity building in Africa. Second, Member States remain free to decide whether to make available troops in a particular situation. Thus, the United Nations is unable to rely on Sates' contributions and has to enter into time-consuming negotiations every time troops are needed.

Nevertheless, the United Nations did successfully intervene in situations of ongoing massive violations of human rights in the Democratic Republic of the Congo, Sierra Leone and East Timor.

The deployment of operation Artemis to Bunia in the Democratic Republic of Congo, from June to September 2003, provides a valuable case study for the capacity and limitations of the United Nations to deploy military in cases of ongoing large-scale violence.

The North-Eastern region of Ituri has a long history of ethnic conflicts over access to land, mineral resources and control of local power. Between 1999 and 2003, approximately 50,000 people were killed in factional fighting and 500,000

283 See for the following *Joachim Koops/ Johannes Varwick*, Ten Years of SHIRBRIG, GPPi Research Paper Series No. 11 (2008).

displaced. The conflict developed increasingly into a proxy war with Uganda, Rwanda and the government in Kinshasa supporting rival factions, including through the delivery of weapons.

Under pressure from the Security Council on all foreign troops to leave the country, the DRC and Uganda signed an agreement in Luanda, on 6 September 2002, which established a timetable for the withdrawal of the Ugandan Defense Forces. At the same time, the Secretary-General had reported to the Security Council on the risks associated with the withdrawal of foreign troops in general, and the severe insecurity, intensified fighting and grave violations of human rights especially in Bunia.[284] The Ugandan troops began withdrawing in late April 2003 and it became clear immediately, that the fragile political process that the United Nations Mission had tried to support after the Luanda Agreement would not be sustainable in the rapidly deteriorating security environment. As the Ugandan withdrawal was carried out in a precipitous and destabilizing manner, the Secretary-General decided to redeploy a Uruguayan battalion from other parts of the country to carry out a limited mandate according to its training and equipment, including static guard duties to ensure the security of United Nations assets and personnel. The protection of civilians was not referred to in the request for redeployment to the government of Uruguay.[285]

As the last Ugandan troops left Bunia on 6 May 2003, Lendu-based militias and the predominantly Hema Union of Congolese Patriots attempted to take control of the town. The streets beyond the UN compounds at a market place in town and at the airport fell under the control of rival militias, who attacked the civilian population perceived as supporting their opponents. Humanitarian agencies and NGOs were forced to evacuate.[286] Reports on large-scale atrocities led to an international outcry about United Nations inaction at the risk of yet another genocide being committed in the Great Lakes Region.

After he had spoken to President Jacques Chirac, who indicated that France would be willing to deploy a force to Bunia, on 15 May 2003, the Secretary-General sent a letter to the Security Council calling for the rapid temporary deployment to Bunia

> of a highly trained and well-equipped multinational force, under the lead of a Member State, to provide security at the airport as well as to other vital installations in the town and to protect the civilian population.[287]

On 30 May, the Security Council authorized the deployment, until 1 September, of an Interim Emergency Multinational Force (IEMF) in Bunia

284 Seventh report of the Secretary-General, U.N.-Doc. S/2001/373 of 17 April 2001, para. 118.

285 See for details Operation Artemis: The Lessons of the Interim Emergency National Force, Peacekeeping Best Practices Unit, Military Division, DPKO, October 2004.

286 See for details Second special report of the Secretary-General, U.N.-Doc. S/2003/566 of 27 May 2004.

287 U.N.-Doc. S/2003/574 of 28 May 2003.

> to contribute to the stabilization of the security conditions and the improvements of the humanitarian situation in Bunia, to ensure the protection of the airport, the internally displaced persons in the camps in Bunia and, if the situation requires it, to contribute to the safety of the civilian population, United Nations personnel and the humanitarian presence in town.[288]

After President Chirac had realized that the original idea of deploying a French-led force was an ideal case to prove the capacity of the European Union to act autonomously from NATO, the operation was renamed Artemis and deployed in the context of the European Defense and Security Policy.

On 6 June 2003, the first forward elements were deployed to Bunia. The total force numbered approximately 1,400, including 220 Special Forces from France and Sweden, with half of the force deployed at headquarters in Entebbe, Uganda. French air assets based in the region provided close air support, reconnaissance and surveillance.

As an initial measure, the force declared the town and a 10 km area around it a 'weapons-invisible' zone and did not tolerate the open carrying of weapons. In different clashes with the militias in June and early July, the force proved its willingness to respond robustly to any challenge to its authority or threats to the security of the population. Ultimately, the force re-established security in Bunia and weakened the military capacity of the rival militias, including through the interception of military supplies. As a result, the political process in Ituri resumed and 60,000 displaced people and refugees returned. Even economic and social activities recovered to a certain extend. After handing over operations to MONUC, the last IEMF elements left Bunia on 7 September 2003.[289]

While operation Artemis was reviewed with a view to the capacity of the European Union to launch military operations, UN-EU cooperation or the planning of future UN peace-keeping missions, the experience offers as well a valuable lesson for the consideration of limited short-term United Nations operations to prevent or halt genocide, war crimes and crimes against humanity in the context of the responsibility to protect. These lessons include the methodology as much as the operational resources employed.[290]

The force responded robustly to any challenge of its authority, but did not use force against one party in particular. In addition, the force seized and confiscated weapons, but did not carry out a comprehensive programme to disarm the militia groups. While weapons were not taken out of circulation and atrocities did occur beyond the very limited area of operation, this approach allowed the force to be perceived as impartial, but not neutral. Furthermore, since the majority of troops were French, they were able to communicate with the local population, which facilitated cooperation and improved intelligence. Through the deployment of a

288 U.N.-Doc. S/RES/1484 (2003) of 30 May 2003.

289 Fourteenth report of the Secretary-General on the United Nations Organization Mission in the Democratic Republic of the Congo, U.N.-Doc. S/2003/1098 of 17 November 2003.

290 See for the following Kees Homan, Operation Artemis in the Democratic Republic of the Congo, in: *European Commission* (ed.), Faster and more united? The debate about Europe's crisis response capacity, May 2007, p. 151 et seq.

civil-military liaison officer along with the first French troops, the force was able to establish dialogue and cooperation with the humanitarian agencies and to benefit from their in-depth knowledge on the ground.

With regard to the operational resources, the proximity of the airbase in Entebbe allowed excellent operational support to the forward base in Bunia. In addition, air assets were very effective for surveillance, reconnaissance and the show of strength. The use of Special Forces gave the mission an effective capability to engage armed threats, even beyond the area of operation. The force also had excellent intelligence capabilities, including the capacity to intercept cellular calls, satellite imagery to track movement of forces and night vision capabilities.

With regard to the consideration of similar missions in the future, it was observed that the very strict insistence on the three-month deployment signaled clearly to the armed militias the transitory nature of the force. The length of deployment should be adequate to allow for the takeover by a more permanent and comprehensive arrangement. In this particular case, following the insistence of France, the Security Council made the expansion of MONUC a de facto condition for the deployment of the IEMF. In other cases, any security vacuum must be prevented. Others observed that the very strict limits on the area of operation pushed the problem of violence against civilians outside the parameters of the forces, where atrocities continued and militias waited out the mission. Overall, the IEMF deployment was considered a success, which, however, manly depended on the ability of MONUC to deploy a capable and robust brigade to take over and extend operations beyond Bunia.[291]

In addition to the lessons provided for special limited short-term missions, the case urges the United Nations to provide in all missions, where a certain risk level of large scale violations of human rights and humanitarian law prevails, for a highly mobile reserve force ready to deploy robustly and rapidly for short periods to stabilize situations and protect United Nations personnel and civilians until a longer term solution can be provided.[292] This lesson is supported by the peacekeeping experience in Sierra Leone in the context of Operation Palliser.

In 1991, civil war broke out in Sierra Leone when the Revolutionary United Front (RUF) launched an insurgency against President Joseph Momoh. Unlike other conflicts, provoked by inter-ethnic or religious strive, the crisis in Sierra Leone was a product of a complex combination of internal and external political factors. The following years were marked by widespread violence, as the rebels used terror, mutilation, rape and torture against the civilian population and the government used mercenaries in attempts to defeat the rebels. After a series of peace accords, in 1999, the Lomé Peace Agreement provided for a comprehensive transition under President Kabbah and the Security Council authorized the United Nations in Sierra Leone

291 Richard Gowan, EUFOR RD Congo, UNIFIL and future European Support to the UN, in: *SDA Discussion Paper*, The AU's Africa Strategy: What are the lessons of the Congo Mission?, Brussels, 2007, p. 29 et seq.

292 Operation Artemis: The Lessons of the Interim Emergency National Force, Peacekeeping Best Practices Unit, Military Division, DPKO, October 2004, p. 7.

(UNAMSIL) to monitor the process of the agreement. However, the ECOWAS Ceasefire Monitoring Group that had been deployed in 1998 withdrew before UNAMSIL reached its full strength creating a security vacuum that the rebels started to exploit. In May 2000, RUF attacked disarmament, demobilization and rehabilitation centers and resisted UNAMSIL deployment to an area where the rebels conducted diamond mining. Two weeks later, 352 UNAMSIL soldiers were presumed to be in the hands of RUF, 25 wounded and fifteen remained missing.[293] At the same time, the rebels unleashed a wave of brutality against the civilian population. International and local media condemned the United Nations and its inability to stop the rampage of the RUF through the country and all the way to its capital.

On 7 May 2000, about 800 United Kingdom troops and a substantial British naval presence offshore were deployed at the airport and in the western part of Freetown with the objective to evacuate British nationals. The force also undertook a large-scale training operation for government security forces providing short-term training to 14,000 troops. Through these activities, it was possible to create a security cordon around Freetown. Furthermore, the presence of the British forces and robust action against the RUF boosted the confidence of the Sierra Leoneans that the United Nations were serious about helping them and enabled UNAMSIL to redeploy much needed troops. The action of British troops also caused fear in the members of RUF. The United Kingdom maintained the presence until UNAMSIL was reinforced and its mandate redefined by the Security Council,

> to deter and where necessary, decisively counter the threat of RUF attacks by responding robustly to any hostile action or threat of imminent and direct use of force.[294]

After the May crisis, UNAMSIL implemented a strategy of negotiation and the progressive demonstration of deterrence, gradually deploying throughout the country with the aim of closing the option of war for the RUF.[295] The success taught the lesson that robust peacekeeping can be an effective deterrent to parties, who might otherwise return to fighting. In addition, the mission maintained continuous dialogue with the parties despite the hostile attitude of the RUF.

Both cases provide evidence that military intervention in favor of vulnerable groups threatened by massive human rights violations can be carried out successfully short of invasion and occupation of the whole country concerned. Deployment in camps and villages, establishment of road blocks or the

293 Fourth report of the Secretary-General on the United Nations Mission in Sierra-Leone, U.N.-Doc. S/2000/455 of 19 May 2000, para. 56 et seq.

294 U.N.-Doc. S/RES/1299 (2000) of 19 May 2000; S/RES/1313 (2000) of 4 August 2000; S/RES/1346 (2001) of 30 March 2001.

295 See for details on the UNAMSIL strategy Peacekeeping best Practices Unit, Lessons Learnt from United Nations Peacekeeping Experience in Sierra Leone, September 2003.

implementation of no-fly zones could be adequate military responses to ongoing violations.[296]

In addition, the United Nations developed a concept of deterrence for particular challenges related to the protection of civilians during ongoing peace keeping operations. In 1993, the Security Council decided

> to extend [...] the mandate of UNPROFOR in order to enable it [...] to deter attacks against the safe areas, to monitor the cease-fire, to promote the withdrawal of military and paramilitary units other than those of the Government of the Republic of Bosnia and Herzegovina and to occupy some key points on the ground, in addition to participating in the delivery of humanitarian relief to the population [...].[297]

While UNPROFOR lacked the capacity to implement its mandate with regard to Srebrenica and the other safe areas, today, the presence of a sufficiently equipped military force has still been used as a means of deterrence of attacks on civilians or humanitarian convoys.[298]

In 2005, following the occupation of Bukavu by mutinous forces of the Congolese Army that resulted in the killing of civilians, MONUC conducted aggressive action in order to force disarmament and pre-empt attacks on civilians.[299] While the impact of this action on the protection of civilians is assessed differently, it provided valuable lessons for future operations and deserves careful review.[300] Finally, preventive deployment was used successfully in Macedonia in 1995.[301]

Traditional peacekeeping often lacks an exit strategy. While this undermines sustainable support from Member States to peacekeeping operations, the risks and resources involved in interventions to implement the responsibility to react will be even more sensitive for national governments and, thus, they require clear benchmarks for the successive transfer of tasks to other actors in order to mobilize political will. In his report on the factors the Security Council should assess in deciding to launch, close or significantly alter a United Nations peacekeeping operation, the Secretary-General underlined the unique circumstances of each

296 See e.g. *Lee Feinstein*, Darfur and Beyond. What is Needed to Prevent Mass Atrocities, Council on Foreign Relations, 22 January 2007; *David Mephan/ Alexander Ransbotham*, Safeguarding Civilians. Delivering on the Responsibility to Protect in Africa, IPPR Report, 2007; Robert Rotberg, How a French-led Force Could Safe Somalia, Financial Times, 12 January 2007.

297 U.N.-Doc. S/RES/836 (1993) of 4 June 1993, para. 5.

298 See most recently Report of the Secretary-General on the United Nations Mission in the Central African Republic and Chad, U.N.-Doc. S/2008/601 of 12 September 2008, para. 65 et seq.

299 See Seventeenth report of the Secretary-General on the United Nations Organization Mission in the Democratic Republic of the Congo, U.N.-Doc. S/2005/167 of 15 March 2005.

300 *Victoria Holt/ Tobias Berkman*, The Impossible Mandate? Military Preparedness, the Responsibility to Protect and Modern Peace Operations, The Henry L. Stimson Center, 2006, p. 167 et seq.

301 See *Henryk Sokalski*, An Ounce of Prevention. Macedonia and the UN Experience in Preventive Diplomacy, United States Institute for Peace, 2003.

conflict that have to be taken into account.[302] At the same time, some of his general conclusions could as well be applied when defining the exit strategy for interventions implementing the responsibility to react. In particular, the Secretary-General underlined that an exit strategy depends on the entrance strategy. The latter would require a joint assessment of the situation within the Security Council and a clear strategy on steps following the intervention. Thus, the exit strategy will dovetail with the initial analysis and recommendations to address a situation through the responsibility to protect.

It can be concluded from past experience that Member States and regional organizations acted on behalf of the United Nations and provided short-term protection of vulnerable groups. Therefore, the mandate and capacities already exist for such tasks. However, with regard to the current discussions on the responsibility to react, concerns prevail with regard to the scope and duration of such operations. National military could prepare better for such tasks if the Secretariat would provide a clear concept for such exceptional operations.

Also the police can play an important role to mitigate violence related to ongoing or imminent genocide, war crimes and crimes against humanity.[303] United Nations Police play a crucial role in UN peace operations since the 1960s; they go on patrol, provide training, advise national policing services, help ensure compliance with human rights standards and assist in a wide range of other areas. Through its activities, UN Police can help to create a safer environment where vulnerable groups will be better protected and criminal activity prevented, disrupted and investigated. In Eastern Slavonia, Kosovo and East Timor, UN police was responsible for interim law enforcement. In these cases, the United Nations could prove that it has the capacity to carry out the authority and responsibility for the maintenance of law and order, including the power of arrest, detention and searches. In addition, members of formed police units supported national law enforcement agencies in the execution of their functions, e.g. in the Democratic Republic of the Congo and Cote d'Ivoire. Through their support for reform, restructuring and rebuilding of national police and law enforcement agencies through training and advising, UN police can influence the dynamics of violent conflict, in particular by countering impunity.

DPKO is currently working on the establishment of a Standing Police Capacity (SPC) of a small number of officers to form rapid response teams suited for the demands of peacekeeping operations. Following the recommendation of the High-level Panel on threats, Challenges and Change[304], the World Summit Outcome document endorsed the creation of a standing police capacity to provide coherent, effective and responsive start-up capabilities for peacekeeping missions and to assist existing missions through the provision of advice and expertise.[305] With regard to

302 No exit without strategy: Security Council decision-making and the closure or transition of United Nations peacekeeping operations, Report of the Secretary-General, U.N. doc. S/2001/394 of 20 April 2001.

303 High-level Panel report, FN. 40, para. 221.

304 Op. cit., para. 223.

305 U.N.-Doc. A/RES/60/1 of 24 October 2005, para. 92

these objectives, the SPC could offer important resources for the United Nations to respond to ongoing or imminent large-scale violence against civilians through the rapid deployment of an effective police presence.[306]

The availability of a United Nations radio facility has been proven very valuable to distribute clear messages to the population on the intentions of the intervention. Military capacities should include jamming radio stations distributing hate messages.[307]

1.2.3 Existing capacities regarding the responsibility to rebuild

The responsibility to rebuild has received very limited attention in discussions so far apart from the agreement that it is an important part of the responsibility to protect.

The ICISS considered the responsibility to protect in the context of military intervention, which should include a genuine commitment to helping to build durable peace, and promoting good governance and sustainable development. This commitment would require sufficient funds and resources and close cooperation with the local population. It may mean staying in the country for some period of time after the initial purpose of the intervention had been accomplished. The ICISS underlined the need for a post-intervention strategy if a military intervention was contemplated. The main objective of such a strategy was to ensure that the reasons for the intervention did not repeat themselves or resurface. In describing the most crucial areas that the responsibility to rebuild must address, the ICISS referred to different immediate, medium-term and long-term measures related to security, justice and reconciliation, and development.[308]

The obligations deriving from the responsibility to rebuild can be established from the general considerations on post-conflict peace building within the United Nations and the lessons-learnt in different country situations throughout the world. The methodologies applied needs to be reviewed for their particular contribution to the prevention of genocide, war crimes and crimes against humanity.

Former Secretary-General Boutros-Ghali defined post-conflict peace building as 'action to identify and support structures which will tend to strengthen and solidify peace in order to avoid a relapse into conflict'.[309] Subsequently, the expression was used rather unspecified to describe short-term to long-term measures within the context of post-conflict recovery. While peace building should be distinguished from peacekeeping, since the 1990s, they are often undertaken simultaneously and within the mandate of an integrated United Nations mission.[310] Peace building

306 See the proposal in High-level Panel report, FN. 40, para. 201.

307 Rwanda report, FN. 259, p. 40

308 ICISS report, FN. 35, p. 39 et seq.

309 An Agenda for Peace, FN. 238, para. 12.

310 See e.g. UNTAG in Namibia (1989-90), ONUSAL in El Salvador (1991-95), UNAVEM II in Angola (1991-95), UNTAC in Cambodia (1991-93), ONUMOZ in Mozambique (1992-94).

activities by the United Nations include drafting or amending of constitutions; implementing disarmament, demobilization and reintegration programs; humanitarian assistance; facilitating transitional justice systems; strengthening state institutions and the delivery of public services; supporting independent civil society and media; reform of the security sector; and organization of elections. In addition to DPKO, UNDP, the Department of Political Affairs (DPA) and some 31 other United Nations agencies, funds and programs are represented in the field and undertake peace building activities. The differences in mandates and approaches required coordination and the development of common strategies.

The Brahimi report made a number of recommendations for peace building in the context of the need of an exit strategy for every peacekeeping mission.[311] Secretary-General Kofi Annan also considered peace building activities in the absence of any military deployment.[312] However, coordination continued to fall short of expectations with a view to the very limited impact of United Nations peace building in the prevention of the recurrence of war and the establishment of functioning and inclusive political institutions.

The High-level panel report discussed post-conflict peace building within the context of collective security and the use of force, after endorsing the responsibility to protect and five basic criteria of legitimacy that the Security Council should address before authorizing military action.[313] With regard to scenarios considered in the context of the responsibility to protect, the panel argued that the mediation and successful implementation of a peace agreement offered hope for breaking long-standing cycles of violence. The panel warned that peace agreements by governments or rebels that engage in or encourage mass human rights abuses had no value and could not be implemented as they raise fundamental opposition. Deploying peace enforcement and peacekeeping forces might be essential in terminating a conflict, but were not sufficient for long-term recovery. The Panel proposed the creation of a single intergovernmental organ dedicated to peace building in all its multiple dimensions.

In his report In Larger Freedom, Secretary-General Kofi Annan recalled that the record of the United Nations in mediating and implementing peace agreements contained some devastating failures as e.g. the genocide in Rwanda occurred after a peace agreement was signed. If the United Nations wanted to prevent conflict, it had to ensure that peace agreements were implemented in a sustainable manner. In order to achieve this end, he proposed to Member States to create an intergovernmental Peace Building Commission.[314] This proposal modified the recommendation of the High-level Panel based on reactions from Member States. In particular, he proposed

311 Brahimi report, FN. 240, para. 35 et seq.

312 See e.g. Implementation of the United Nations Millennium Declaration. Report of the Secretary-General, U.N.-Doc. A/58/323 of 2 September 2003, para. 40.

313 High-level Panel report, FN. 40, para. 221 et seq.

314 In Larger Freedom report, FN. 44, para. 114 et seq.

a prevention role of the Commission in order to avert situations from relapsing into war within the first five to ten years after the signing of a peace agreement.[315]

The World Summit Outcome document provided for agreements on peace building in the context of peace and collective security,[316] while the responsibility to protect was considered in the context of human rights and the rule of law. Unfortunately, the emphasis on conflict prevention as proposed by the Secretary-General and the High-level panel was omitted from further discussion, most likely by powerful Member States fearful of limiting the Security Council's primary role in the area of peace and security. The focus on the post conflict dimension of peace building limited as well the role that the Commission could have played in the development of a continuum of steps in the context of the responsibility to protect by linking the responsibility to rebuild to the other two dimensions.[317]

The mandate of the Peace Building Commission[318] reflects the agreement of Member States with regard to the importance of sustainable peace for conflict prevention and a desire to prevent situations similar to Rwanda in 1994, when the General Assembly established the Commission

> Recognizing that development, peace and security and human rights are interlinked and mutually reinforcing,
>
> Emphasizing the need for a coordinated, coherent and integrated approach to post-conflict peacebuilding and reconciliation with a view to achieving sustainable peace [...].

However, the role of the Peace Building Commission in implementing the responsibility to rebuild after military intervention might be limited by its relationship with the Security Council. The General Assembly

> Underlines that in post-conflict situations on the agenda of the Security Council with which it is actively seized, in particular when there is a United Nations-mandated peacekeeping mission on the ground or under way and given the primary responsibility of the Council for the maintenance of international peace and security in accordance with the Charter, the main purpose of the Commission will be to provide advice to the Council at its request [...].

During its first year of work, the Commission considered Burundi and Sierra Leone. Both countries could offer valuable lessons for addressing root causes of large-scale violence with a view to define obligations of Member States and the international community within the responsibility to rebuild. However, the deliberations of the Commission were limited mainly on the general conflict prevention considerations rather than the prevention of genocide, war crimes and crimes against humanity in this context.

In addition, the Commission established a Working Group on Lessons Learnt to accumulate best practices on critical peace building issues. The primary objective of the Working Group has been to contribute to the country specific deliberations of

315 Op. cit., paras. 2, 16 et seq.

316 Summit Outcome document, FN. 16, para. 97 et seq.

317 *Richard Ponzio*, The United Nations Peacebuilding Commission: origins and initial practice, Disarmament Forum 2007, no. 2, p. 5 et seq.

318 See for the following U.N.-Doc. A/RES/60/180 of 30 December 2005.

the Commission.[319] However, the Working Group could include in its agenda discussions on specific lessons related to large-scale human rights violations and seek the advice of, inter alia, the Special Adviser on the Prevention of Genocide and the High Commissioner for Human Rights.[320]

Upon request by the General Assembly and the Security Council, the United Nations launched the Peacebuilding Fund on 11 October 2006.[321] The Fund is a global multi-donor trust fund that provides a flexible mechanism for the provision of immediate short-term support during the early stages of a peace process and, under its emergency window, can be made available to any country in exceptional circumstances and that is at risk of lapsing or relapsing into conflict.[322] Currently, the Peacebuilding Fund emergency window is supporting projects in seven countries, including Liberia, Burundi and Kenya.[323] The emergency window of the Fund would allow the Secretary-General a flexible and fast response to support the implementation of the responsibility to rebuild in a strategic and forward-looking way.

While a comprehensive review of possible United Nations action with regard to the implementation of the responsibility to rebuild would be beyond the scope of this publication, the capacity of the United Nations will be considered with regard to the most imminent challenges after large-scale human rights violations took place, i.e. the provision of physical security to all members of society, the establishment of basic mechanisms for accountability and justice, and access to basic social services and economic and social rights.[324] Furthermore the crucial task of demobilization as a critical condition for democratization, justice and development should be mentioned in this context.

With regard to the provision of physical security the immediate deployment of an international presence to protect vulnerable groups and individuals will be necessary. In this regard, the civilian, military and police capacities considered in

319 Report of the Peacebuilding Commission on its first session, U.N.-Doc. A/62/137 – S/2007/458 of 25 July 2007.

320 See for more general suggestions on opportunities for the PBC *Thomas J. Biersteker*, Prospects for the UN Peacebuilding Commission, Disarmament Forum, 2007, no. 2, p. 37 et seq.

321 U.N.-Doc. A/RES/60/180 of 12 September 2005; U.N.-Doc. S/RES/1645 (2005) of 20 December 2005.

322 Arrangements for establishing the Peacebuilding Fund. Report of the Secretary-General, U.N.-Doc. A/60/984 of 22 August 2006.

323 See for details on the activities of the Fund The Peacebuilding Fund. Report of the Secretary-General, U.N.-Doc. A/63/218 – S/2008/522 of 4 August 2008.

324 The Special Adviser on the Prevention of Genocide has found that both in the short and in the long-term, the prevention of genocide seems predicated on acting comprehensively in four interrelated areas: (1) physical protection of populations at risk, (2) establishment of accountability for violations of human rights and humanitarian law, (3) access to basic economic, social and cultural rights, (4) support of steps to address underlying causes of conflict. See Report of the Secretary-General on the implementation of the Five Point Action Plan and the activities of the Special Adviser on the Prevention of Genocide, U.N.-Doc. E/CN.4/2006/84 of 1 February 2006, para. 9.

the context of the responsibility to react again come into play. However, as past experience in Rwanda and Kosovo has shown, it will be necessary to provide for contingency to prevent reverse ethnic cleansing and revenge killings in the immediate aftermath of a military intervention.

The establishment of basic mechanisms of accountability and justice should concentrate initially on the implementation of criminal law. The generic criminal code developed by the United Nations offers a framework for immediate implementation. However, the criminal code should be reviewed on a case-by-case basis with a view to fulfill the preventive and deterrent function of criminal law in the context of the country concerned and the analysis of the causes for genocide, war crimes and crimes against humanity in this regard.

Furthermore, it would be important for the United Nations presence to show its determination to provide accountability for genocide, war crimes and crimes against humanity.[325] Mindful of the experience that in the aftermath of a violent conflict there is often only a small window of opportunity to gather evidence, some Member States sought to fill some of the existing gaps through the Justice Rapid Response (JRR) initiative. JRR is based on loose intergovernmental cooperation and aims at responding quickly to requests for expertise and resources in support of genuine efforts to identify, collect and preserve information about genocide, war crimes and crimes against humanity.[326] This initiative would enable the United Nations or the government concerned to request urgent assistance in the immediate aftermath of a military intervention.

Access to basic economic, social and cultural rights will include humanitarian aid to victims, displaced persons and refugees. However, in the context of genocide, war crimes and crimes against humanity often the displacement and lack of access to basic social services are part of the pattern to commit such crimes. Therefore, it will be necessary for immediate measures to discontinue these patterns. In this regard, the United Nations would require emergency packages for immediate implementation of critical projects, depending on the circumstances prevailing in the country concerned. However, notwithstanding the different circumstances, previous situations have shown that revisions in property law, housing rights, employment regulations, basic social services and access to reconstruction assistance would be areas where United Nations action might be needed immediately after a military intervention.

There is a wealth of experience, methodology and lessons available within different United Nations departments, agencies and funds on the strengthening of the

325 Anja Seibert-Fohr, Reconstruction through Accountability, in: *Armin von Bogdandy/ Rüdiger Wolfrum* (eds.), Max Planck Yearbook of United Nations Law, Volume 9, 2005, p. 555 et seq.

326 Justice Rapid Response Feasibility Study, October 2005, available at http://www.auswaertiges-amt.de/diplo/en/Aussenpolitik/InternatRecht/IStGh/IStGH-JRRdownload.pdf.

rule of law in post-conflict societies.[327] Rule of law and transitional justice issues are now being consistently integrated into the strategic and operational planning of new peace operations.[328] However, the expertise and experience available require systematic review and strategic development in order to respond to the needs of Member States.[329] The inventory of rule of law activities of the United Nations provides a valuable basis for this review and an example to follow for other activities relevant for the implementation of the responsibility to protect, including human rights and humanitarian support.[330]

In 2007, DPKO created the Office of the Rule of Law and Security Institutions to provide an integrated and forward-looking approach to United Nations assistance in this area. The Office unifies police, judicial, legal and correctional units as well as mine action, disarmament, demobilization and reintegration, and security sector reform, primarily in support of peacekeeping operations.[331] The Office could make an important contribution in collecting and developing means to reinforcing rule of law and establishing security after military intervention in situations of genocide, war crimes and crimes against humanity.

1.2.4 Conclusions

The application of the responsibility to protect requires a systematic approach, based on priorities defining a continuum of measures, including prevention, reaction and rebuilding. With a view to the inherent assessment of a situation as exceptional, the United Nations cannot continue business as usual, while the same methodologies and approaches might remain applicable. The identification of those measures applicable in particular in situations of imminent or ongoing genocide, war crimes and crimes against humanity will make an important contribution to the creation of political will of the Member States to agree on such a continuum that, ultimately, might lead to military intervention.

327 See The rule of law and transitional justice in conflict and post-conflict societies. Report of the Secretary-General, U.N.-Doc. S/2004/616 of 23 August 2004.

328 See for details Uniting our strengths: Enhancing United Nations support for the rule of law. Report of the Secretary-General, U.N.-Doc. A/61/636 – S/2006/980 of 14 December 2006.

329 See S/PRST/2003/15 of 24 September 2003.

330 See The rule of law at the national and international levels. Report of the Secretary-General, U.N.-Doc. A/63/64 of 12 March 2008.

331 See Security peace and development: the role of the United Nations in supporting security sector reform. Report of the Secretary-General, U.N.-Doc. A/62/659 – S/2008/39 of 23 January 2008.

2. *Possible contributions by regional organizations and civil society*

2.1 Regional Organizations

The World Summit Outcome document provided for the responsibility of the international community to use appropriate diplomatic, humanitarian and other peaceful means, including in accordance with Chapter VIII of the Charter, to help to protect people from genocide, war crimes and crimes against humanity. Therefore, the role of regional organizations in the operationalization of the responsibility to protect has to be considered in detail. In practice, the United Nations has cooperated with regional arrangements and agencies in situations relevant for the development and application of the concept, including Darfur, Kosovo, Somalia and Srebrenica.

According to Chapter VIII of the Charter, the contribution of regional agreements and organizations to the settlement of local disputes is legal, while the ultimate responsibility for the maintenance of international peace and security maintains with the Security Council.[332] While the exact meaning of the terms used in article 52 of the Charter remains disputed, Secretary-General Boutros-Ghali urged Member States to strengthen regional cooperation on the maintenance of peace and security and broadened the circle of organizations that legally could take dispute settlement action from the Organization of American States, the African Union and the League of Arab States to include the Association of South-East Asian Nations and the Organization for Security and Cooperation in Europe.[333] Other organizations that have been considered in this context include the European Union and the Economic Community of West African States (ECOWAS).[334]

There is a range of activities related to conflict prevention that could be carried out by regional organizations in cooperation with the United Nations in cases of imminent or ongoing mass atrocities.[335] They could develop a range of measures, tactics and sanctions in support of United Nations action to implement the responsibility to protect.[336] However, regional organizations will be considered in the following mainly from the perspective of cooperating partners as far as they provide for regional rapid reaction in cases of mass atrocities. Furthermore, the experience of regional organizations in establishing and operating response capacity for intervention in situations of imminent or ongoing large-scale violence provides

332 Hummer/ Schweizer, Article 52, in: *Simma*, FN. 97, para. 11.

333 An Agenda for Peace, FN. 238, para. 61 et seq.

334 Hummer/ Schweizer, op. cit., para. 89 et seq.

335 See e.g. U.N.-Doc. S/RES/1809 (2008) of 16 April 2008 adopted following a high-level debate of the Security-Council on the cooperation with regional organizations. Summary of the debate in Press Release SC/9301.

336 See Implementing the Responsibility to Protect: The Role of Regional and Sub-Regional Partners, Report on Wilton Park Conference 922, 2008.

valuable lessons-learnt for the development of a United Nations capacity. It appears from research in this issue that only a few multinational organizations can employ force for more than self-defense: NATO, the European Union, the African Union and ECOWAS. All of these organizations are still developing a concept of operations for the civilian protection and clear guidance for their forces participating in operations in the particular environment of imminent or ongoing genocide, war crimes and crimes against humanity.[337]

2.1.1 The European Union (EU)

At the European Council in Cologne, in 1999, the European Union committed itself to take decisions on the full range of conflict prevention and management tasks, including the 'Petersberg tasks' of the Western European Union, i.e. humanitarian and rescue tasks, peace-keeping and combat forces in crisis management, including peace-making. Consequently, the European Council held in Helsinki later that year agreed on new political and military bodies to be created within the Council.[338]

So far, the European Union deployed five military missions to Bosnia and Herzegovina, Chad/ Central African Republic, twice to the Democratic Republic of the Congo and to Macedonia.[339] As mentioned above, operation Artemis was deployed in a situation where civilians faced ongoing attacks. The European Union does not provide for any written military doctrine, in the traditional sense, for forces participating in European Union operations. The Union may commit itself to improving its capacities before it identifies specific missions, including missions that view the protection of civilians as a specific objective within the responsibility to protect.

Since 2007, EU Member States provided for two battle groups of 1,500 troops each that can be deployed within ten days in a radius of 6,000 km around Brussels. Battle groups will implement the tasks listed in article 17, paragraph 2 of the Treaty on the European Union and in the European Security Strategy, in particular tasks of combat forces in crisis management.[340] The capabilities of the battle groups have been illustrated by five scenarios, including conflict prevention, separation of parties by force, stabilization, reconstruction and military advice to third countries, evacuation operations and assistance to humanitarian operations. The battle groups

337 See for details *Victoria Holt*, The military and civilian protection: developing roles and capacities, HPG Report 21, p. 53-66.

338 Hummer/ Schweitzer, op. cit., para. 90.

339 http://www.consilium.europa.eu/cms3_fo/showPage.asp?id=268&lang=EN

340 Article 17, paragraph 2, of the Treaty on the European Union as amended by the Treaty of Nice provides that the common foreign and security policy shall 'include humanitarian and rescue tasks, peacekeeping tasks and tasks of combat forces in crisis management, including peacemaking.' See Treaty of Nice Amending the Treaty on European Union, the Treaties Establishing the European Communities And Certain Related Acts, Official Journal C 80, 10 March 2001.

are sustainable for 30 days in initial operations, extendable to 120 days, if supplied appropriately.[341]

The United Nations has welcomed the idea of a rapidly-deployable battle group as either a bridging force to help the United Nations prepare a new mission or expand an existing one, or as a reserve force to respond under a UN mandate to contingencies beyond the capacity of the United Nations itself. However, according to article 25 of the Treaty on the European Union, full political control of EU forces must remain at all times with the Political and Security Committee.[342] The EU and the United Nations increased progressively the institutional relationship between the Council of the European Union, DPKO and DPA.[343] The most recent cooperation between the European Union and the United Nations on elections in the DRC mission and the deployment of United Nations Mission in the Central African Republic and Chad (MINURCAT) could offer valuable lessons as well for cooperation in situations of mass atrocities.

2.1.2 The African Union (AU)

The Constitutive Act of the African Union of 2002 merged the Organization of African Unity and the African Economic Community with the aim of strengthening solidarity among African countries.[344] Article 4 (h) of the Constitutive Act includes among the principles of the Union

> [t]he right of the Union to intervene in a Member State [...] in respect of grave circumstances, namely war crimes, genocide and crimes against humanity.[345]

African leaders, like the former Chairman of the African Union Commission, Alpha Oumar Konare, advocated that the African Union moved away from a culture of non-intervention to a culture of non-indifference.[346] Some argued that the African Union had the responsibility to protect citizens in African from human rights atrocities, even if the wording of the Constitutive Act might be different from the World Summit Outcome document.

In implementation of the principle, article 7 (e) of the Protocol of the Peace and Security Council provides that the latter can

341 See for more details EU Council Secretariat, Factsheet, EU Battlegroups, February 2008.

342 See for details Thierry Tardy, EU-UN cooperation in Peacekeeping: A Promising Relationship in a Constrained Environment, in: *Martin Ortega* (ed.), The European Union and the United Nations, Chaillot Paper 78, Paris, 2005, p. 49 et seq.

343 See for details *Alexandra Novosseloff*, EU-UN Partnership in Crisis Management. Developments and Prospects, New York, 2004.

344 Hummer/ Schweitzer, op. cit., para. 69.

345 See in more general *Peter Harrell*, Modern-day 'Guarantee Clauses' and the Legal Authority of Multinational Organizations to Authorize the Use of Military Force, 33 Yale J. Int'l L. 417.

346 *Tim Murhiti*, The responsibility to protect, as enshrined in article 4 of the Constitutive Act of the African Union, African Security Review 16.2, p. 15.

recommend to the Assembly of Heads of State intervention, on behalf of the Union, in a Member State in respect of grave circumstances, namely war crimes, genocide and crimes against humanity, as defined in relevant international conventions and instruments.

The Common African Defense and Security Policy is based on the principle of interdependence.[347]

The African Union decided to establish an African Standby Force by 2010 to cooperate with the United Nations and sub regional African organizations in conducting peace operations. The Force will be comprised of one brigade of 3,000 to 5,000 troops from each of the five sub regions.[348] An early-warning system will be established[349] and a Panel of the Wise will assist with preventing the outbreak or escalation of conflict[350]. In support of AU activities, the United Nations decided to support the establishment of institutional and operational capacities.[351]

With regard to the implementation of the principle, the AU deployment to Burundi, Darfur and Somalia provide valuable examples and lessons-learnt for future cooperation with the United Nations and the requirements of any international presence in situations of imminent or ongoing violence. It can be concluded from this experience that the African Union troops have been used to deploy in situations of ongoing or imminent violence and carry out a range of activities, including the protection of key personalities, in circumstances where the United Nations did not consider the situation appropriate for the deployment of a peacekeeping mission. With a view to the relationship of the United Nations and the African Union regarding military operations in Darfur and Somalia, the AU risks to be used as political placeholder for robust interventions, when the Security Council lacks political commitment to authorize Member States to act on behalf of the United

347 See Solemn Declaration on A Common African Defense and Security Policy of 28 February 2004.

348 African Union, Roadmap for the Operationalization of the African Standby Force, Annex A-3, Experts' Meeting on the Relationship between the AU and Regional Mechanisms for Conflict Prevention, Management and Resolution, Addis Ababa, 23 March 2005; African Union, Policy Framework for the Establishment of the African Standby Force and the Military Staff Committee, Part I, Document adopted by the Third Meeting of African Chiefs of Defense Staff, Addis Ababa, 15/ 16 May 2003. See for details *Jakkie Cilliers*, The African Standby Force: An Update on Progress, ISS Paper 160, 2008.

349 In 2003, the Intergovernmental Authority on Development (IGAD) established a regional Conflict Early Warning and Response System (CEWARN) with Conflict Early Warning Units (CEWERU) in different countries. So far, ECOWARN for West Africa has been established as an operations center only.

350 In January 2007, Salim Ahmed Salim, former Secretary-General of the OAU, Brigaia Bam, Chairman of the Independent Electoral Commission of South Africa, Ahmed Bed Bella, former President of Algeria, Elisabeth Pognon, President of the Constitutional Court of Benin and Miguel Trovoada, former President of São Tomé and Principe, were nominated for the Panel of the Wise for a period of three years.

351 See U.N.-Doc. A/RES/61/296 of 17 September 2007; Declaration: Enhancing UN-AU Cooperation. Framework for the Ten-Year Capacity-Building Programme for the African Union, U.N.-Doc. A/61/630/Add. of 12 December 2006.

Nations, however, without providing the necessary resources. In addition, the organizations risk to be played off against each other.

While the African Union showed the political resolution to act, it has lacked the appropriate resources to implement effectively robust mandates in different African countries.[352] Some of the mandates provided to the African Union operations, such as the African Union Mission in Sudan (AMIS), are not sufficiently strong to implement the principle expressed in article 4 (h) of the Constitutive Act. Furthermore, the lack of resources provided to the African Union operations is an expression of lack of commitment to regional cooperation, as huge domestic defense budgets are financed by African governments.[353] At the same time, the lack of adequate mandates and resources is an expression by its Member States of the lack of systematic cooperation between the Security Council and the African Union with a view to identifying tasks, indicators and timelines for a hand-over of operations to the United Nations. While the United Nations Assistance Cells in Addis Ababa for the support of the African Union Mission in Somalia (AMISOM) and, previously, AMIS, provided some improvement on the operational and logistic side, much remains to be done, if the AU is expected to stand-in for the United Nations in the future as well.[354]

2.1.3 The Economic Community of West African States (ECOWAS)

A former force commander of the Monitoring Group of the Economic Community of West African States (ECOMOG) claimed that ECOWAS carried out successful intervention missions in cases of ongoing mass atrocities securing a cease-fire, creating an atmosphere conducive to negotiations and protecting non-combatants through the establishment of safe havens.[355]

ECOMOG is a military force formed by member states of ECOWAS from units of their national armed forces. The Protocol on Non-Aggression on the one hand and the Protocol Relating to the Mutual Assistance on Defense on the other provide the legal basis for a non-standing intervention force for a collective response in cases, where a member state was a victim of internal armed conflict that was supported from the outside and was likely to endanger peace and security in the region.[356]

In 1990, ECOMOG intervened in Liberia on the basis of an invitation of the government without prior authorization of the Security Council. ECOWAS acted

352 Report of the Secretary-General on the relationship between the United Nations and regional organizations, in particular the African Union, in the maintenance of international peace and security, U.N.-Doc. S/2008/186 of 7 April 2008.

353 *Murhiti*, FN. 346, p. 15, 23.

354 *Victoria Holt/ Maria Shanahan*, African Capacity-Building for Peace Operations: UN collaboration with the African Union and ECOWAS, Washington D.C., 2005.

355 *Mitikishe Maxwell Khobe*, The Evolution and Conduct of ECOMOG Operations in West Africa, ISS Monograph No. 44: Boundaries of Peace Support Operations, (2000).

356 Quoted from ref. in Hummer/ Schweitzer, op. cit., para. 94.

undoubtedly as regional arrangement or agency according to Chapter VIII, but might not represent a good example for systematic cooperation between the United Nations and regional organizations.[357] Nevertheless, the experience of ECOMOG could provide important lessons for future interventions within the context of the responsibility to protect. Referring to Liberia and Sierra Leone, the former force commander argued that the inability of ECOMOG to secure the consent of all parties prior to the intervention did not make it illegitimate as the conduct of the rebel forces and their attitude to ignore agreements shortly after signing did not leave any other option. In his assessment, all ECOMOG interventions have been successful so far and the troops were subsequently involved in monitoring and enforcing the cease fire they have helped to agree upon.

2.1.4 North Atlantic Treaty Organization (NATO)

Already in January 1994, Heads of State and Government had reiterated their previous offer to support United Nations peace operations on a case-by-case basis.[358] In April 1999, the North Atlantic Council approved the Alliance's new Strategic Concept.[359] The Heads of State and Government acknowledged that '[t]he dangers of the Cold War have given way to more promising, but also challenging prospects, to new opportunities and risks' and decided on the possibility of 'non-Article 5 crisis response operations', i.e. peacekeeping and other operations under the authority of the Security Council, including by making available Alliance resources and expertise.[360] In a section on 'Protection of Humanitarian Operations', the Concept even talks of the possibility of troops operating in the midst of genocide. NATO doctrine also includes various mission tasks that are potentially applicable to civilian protection such as the imposition of no-fly zones, the establishment and supervision of protected or safe areas, and the creation of safe corridors for the passage of civilians and for aid.

Notwithstanding the recommendation of the High-level Panel on the cooperation with the Alliance, so far, the relationship between NATO and the United Nations has not been formalized in official declarations or agreements.[361] United Nations Member States are skeptical about cooperation with a view to NATO intervention in Kosovo without authorization by the Security Council. Furthermore, the discussion in the United States to expand NATO's mandate and membership to an 'Alliance of

357 Hummer/ Schweitzer, op. cit., para. 95 et seq.

358 Declaration of the Heads of State and Government, Ministerial Meeting of the North Atlantic Council/ North Atlantic Cooperation Council, NATO, Brussels, Press Communiqué M-1(94)3 of 11 January 1994.

359 Contained in Press Release NAC-S (99)65 of 24 April 1999.

360 Ibid., para. 31.

361 High-level Panel report, FN. 40, para. 273.

Democracies' increased fear of a competition between the two organizations.[362] At the same time, many United Nations Member States signed bi-lateral agreements with NATO on closer cooperation and conflict resolution. Secretary-General Ban Ki-moon's initiative to arrive at a framework agreement with NATO could benefit from a connection with the responsibility to protect. In 23 September 2008, NATO and the United Nations signed a declaration of cooperation at the margins of the 63rd session of the General Assembly that provoked strong reactions from Russia.[363]

2.2 Civil Society

Civil society plays an important role in the implementation and development of the responsibility to protect.

The contribution of civil society to the prevention or halting of mass atrocities has been recognized in different situations.[364] National and international NGOs present in the country at-risk are important partners for the implementation of preventive and reactive measures by the United Nations.[365] In particular, local civil society organizations can provide the perspective of the population, the victims and other vulnerable groups. In addition, NGOs can provide valuable information and analysis about actors, causes and motives involved in a conflict.

It is important to include the voice of civil society and the population at large in the discussion on the operationalization of the responsibility to protect. Ultimately, the crimes in question are committed by or with the abstention of, governments against the civilian population of their own country. Therefore, it should not come as a surprise that authoritative governments exercising high levels of suppression of large parts of their population are not supporting the idea of a common responsibility to protect. Often, internal conflict shapes the position of Member States in the Security Council and their willingness to intervene in other countries. It has been claimed repeatedly that the rejection by China and Russia to intervene in a country situation was related to the situation in Tibet and Chechnya respectively.

In this regard, the initiative of the WFM to organize regional conferences of civil society on the responsibility to protect could make an important contribution to the discussion about cultural or religious concerns in some regions, provided that the

362 See e.g. *Ivo Badder/ James Goldgeier*, Global NATO, Foreign Affairs, Vol. 85, 2006, Nr. 5, p. 105 et seq.

363 Steve Gutterman, Russia official blasts ‚secretive' UN-NATO deal, The Associated Press, 9 October 2008.

364 See e.g. *Judy Large*, The War Next Door: A Study of Second-Track Interventions During the War in Ex-Yugoslavia (1997); Mohammed Omar Maundi, Preventing Conflict Escalation in Burundi, in: *Chandra Lekha Sriram/ Karin Wermester* (eds.), From Promise to Practice. Strengthening UN Capacities for the Prevention of Violent Conflict (2003), p. 327 et seq.

365 See above C 1.2.2.1

dialogue among civil society can be inclusive and open.[366] It will be important to reach out systematically to regions and countries perceived as skeptical towards the concept in order to further a joint understanding and develop a minimum common denominator as a basis for the operationalization of the responsibility to protect.

The Global Center for the Responsibility to Protect entered into agreements with a number of Associated Centers worldwide with a view to link related research and bring regional perspective to the discussion on implementation.[367] In addition, the Responsibility to Protect – Engaging Civil Society project (R2PCS) provides regular updates on recent developments and an archive of reference material.[368]

Finally, civil society could be an important partner in the advocacy of the responsibility to protect by explaining its origins, limits and challenges to a broader audience on the national and international level.

3. *Case studies*

Since the publication of the Summit Outcome document, different county situations have been considered for the application of the responsibility to protect. In the following, three of those situations will be reviewed in more detail with a view to deduct lessons for the operationalization of the responsibility to protect.

3.1 Darfur

3.1.1 United Nations action

The history and causes of the conflict in Darfur have been analyzed and presented in numerous reports and studies since the situation reached the attention of international media in early 2003.[369] The reaction of the United Nations was concentrated first at the Commission on Human Rights, which sent different fact-finding missions in 2003 and 2004.[370] The Security Council became involved in the

366 See for more details Building an NGO Coalition on R2P: R2PCS holds global consultative roundtables on the Responsibility to Protect, available at http://www.responsibilitytoprotect.org/

367 See for details: http://www.globalr2p.org/centres.html

368 Loc. cit.

369 See e.g. *Julie Flint/ Alex de Waal*, Darfur: A Short History of a Long War (2006); *Alex de Waal* (ed.), War in Darfur and the Search for Peace (2007).

370 See e.g. Report of the United Nations High Commissioner for Human Rights and Follow-Up to the World Conference on Human Rights, Situation of human rights in the Darfur region of the Sudan, U.N.-Doc. E/CN.4/2005/3 of 7 May 2004.

situation in the context of its considerations of the conflict between the Government of Sudan and the Sudan People's Liberation Army/ Movement in the South, which was finally ended by the Comprehensive Peace Agreement concluded in Naivasha with some implications for Darfur, in January 2005. Since mid-2004, in a series of resolutions and Presidential Statements, the Security Council tried to support a political solution for the different causes underlying the conflict between the government and different armed rebel groups.[371] At the same time, the African Union deployed a small number of soldiers in order to monitor the cease-fire entered into in early 2004. Countless foreign ministers and high-level United Nations officers, including the Secretary-General, the High Commissioner for Human Rights and the Special Adviser on the Prevention of Genocide, traveled to Darfur and returned with a similar assessment of the situation and the need for the Government of Sudan to take urgent measures to protect their people from genocide, war crimes and crimes against humanity. In the course of the last four years, the Security Council demanded that the Government of Sudan disarm the Janjaweed, bring the perpetrators of violations of human rights and humanitarian law to justice, established an International Commission of Inquiry to determine whether genocide has occurred, referred the situation in Darfur to the International Criminal Court and established the United Nations Assistance Mission in Darfur (UNAMID). Notwithstanding these activities and the signing of a Darfur Peace Agreement between the Government and one faction of one rebel group in Abuja in May 2006, the situation of the civilian population in Darfur did not improve.[372]

The early reports by the fact-finding missions mandated by the Commission on Human Rights established what is known since as the main pattern of human rights violations in Darfur. Arab tribal militias, armed by the central government in Khartoum since the beginning of the 1990s, have been recruited to fight in counterinsurgency operations against armed rebel groups from Darfur. This Arab militia became known as 'Janjaweed' as they attacked villages across Darfur concentrating on Fur, Masalit and Zaghawa tribal groups from which most of the rebels have been drawn. Many of the attacks have been carried out jointly with regular Sudanese army units and air forces. During the attacks, men, women and children have been killed indiscriminately, villages have been destroyed, livestock stolen or killed, crops burnt and wells poisoned. Rape and sexual assault have been widespread and systematic, including of young girls, breaking down families and communities. Conservative estimates arrive at 2.4 million displaced and 300,000

371 See in particular resolutions 1769 (2007) of 31 July 2007, 1706 (2006) of 31 August 2006, 1679 (2006) of 16 May 2006, 1665 (2006) of 29 March 2006, 1663 (2006) of 24 March 2006, 1593 (2005) of 31 March 2005, 1591 (2005) of 29 March 2005, 1590 (2005) of 24 March 2005, 1574 (2004) of 19 November 2004, 1564 (2004) of 18 September 2004 and 1556 (2004) of 30 July.

372 See for an analysis of the Peace Agreement e.g. International Crisis Group, Darfur's Fragile Peace Agreement, Africa Briefing No. 39, 20 June 2006; for the assessment of the current situation in Darfur see e.g. Report of the Secretary-General on the deployment of the African Union-United Nations Hybrid Operation in Darfur, U.N.-Doc. S/2008/443 of 7 July 2008.

killed. Once people have arrived in camps, they suffer in general from the consequences of varying access of humanitarian agencies due to attacks on aid convoys, killing and kidnapping of humanitarian workers, visa restrictions, customs obstacles and the challenges caused by the climate and landscape of Darfur. In particular, women leaving the vicinity of the camps to undertake farming or search for firewood or grass have been constantly attacked and raped. Responsibility for the insecurity in and around camps has been shared by the Sudanese police, military, Janjaweed, rebels and criminal elements. Apart from the suffering that can be expressed in particular violations of human rights and humanitarian law or statistics contained in humanitarian situation reports, in the camps the family and tribal structures developed over centuries to secure survival in the challenging environment of Darfur are eroding within a climate of impunity, insecurity, sexual violence and dependency on humanitarian aid.[373]

The question of genocide was raised early and publicly, including within the United Nations.[374] In his address to the Commission on Human Rights at the occasion of a special session marking the tenth anniversary of the beginning of the genocide in Rwanda, on 7 April 2004, Secretary-General Kofi Annan stated that reports from Sudan filled him with foreboding that a similar tragedy could happen in Darfur. Five months later, based on interviews of 1,100 refugees from Darfur residing in camps in Chad, US Secretary of State, Colin Powell, told the Senate Foreign Relations Committee that genocide has been committed in Darfur. Returning from a mission to Darfur in September 2005, the Special Adviser on the Prevention of Genocide told the United Nations press corps about his concerns regarding the situation in Darfur, after the Security Council had decided not to invite him to report.[375] Human rights monitors have been deployed to Darfur in mid-2004 and, so far, the High Commissioner has issued ten periodic reports in addition to the regular reporting on the human rights situation through UNMIS and the African Union/ United Nations hybrid operation in Darfur (UNAMID).[376] All these and other mechanisms have concluded that war crimes and crimes against humanity are committed in Darfur on a regular basis.

However, when discussing the application of the responsibility to protect on the situation in Darfur, even prominent supporters reject the idea. Arguments range from non-retroactivity of the concept on situations before 2005 to the argument that

373 See the very instructive study on the consequences of the conflict for the former population of three villages reportedly attacked by Janjaweed and Sudanese military in 2004 in: *Physicians for Human Rights*, Darfur – Assault on Survival. A Call for Security, Justice and Restitution (2006).

374 *Gerard Prunier*, Darfur: The Ambiguous Genocide, Cornell University Press, Ithaca, 2005.

375 Department of Public Information, Press Conference by Special Adviser on Prevention of Genocide, 10 October 2005; Juan E. Mendez, Possibilities for Genocide Prevention, in: *Agnes van Ardenne – van der Hoeven/ Mohammad Salih/ Nick Grono* (eds.), Explaining Darfur: Four Lectures on the Ongoing Genocide, Amsterdam (2007), p. 49 et seq.

376 Available at http://www.ohchr.org/EN/Countries/AfricaRegion/Pages/SDPeriodicReports.aspx

Darfur already developed too much 'down the road' of conflict for the responsibility to protect to be applicable. These arguments raise concerns regarding their substance as much as their negative effect on the acceptance of the responsibility to protect.

First, the argument supports the perception that the responsibility to protect is a norm with negative effect on governments so that it cannot be applied retroactively. This runs against the idea to define the responsibility to protect as a continuum of steps to implement existing legal obligations and concentrating on the potential victims rather than the right of intervention against the government.

Second, the argument reveals the perception that the discussion on Darfur comes at a time when the responsibility to protect is mainly rejected as a disguise of military intervention, while support is stronger for its prevention and capacity-building aspects. However, this line of argument contributes to the insecurity of Member States about the application of the responsibility to protect rather than creating trust in the intentions of the supporters. This position has provoked questions about any added value of the responsibility to protect, if it could not even make any positive impact on the situation in Darfur.

Furthermore, the argument neglects the experience in the past that many situations will already be 'mid-stream' when the attention of the Security Council could be raised. It is in the imminent situations of violence where the responsibility to protect will add most value. There is no particular need for the reconsideration of long-term preventive activities, institution building and capacity building under the lense of the responsibility to protect. Existing concepts, such as the implementation of human rights obligations and conflict prevention measures offer a sufficient framework. Such activities are ongoing in Darfur with no decisive impact on the pattern allegedly constituting genocide, war crimes and crimes against humanity. In addition, this interpretation of the responsibility to protect also unintentionally enforces the perception that double standards prevail and the concept will be applied primarily on developing countries which need support in long-term prevention. If the concept was useful and added value it must be applicable to all stages of a conflict and in all regions of the world.

The assessment of any positive impact of a military intervention in the situation in Darfur should be kept separate from the application of the responsibility to protect. Depending on the analysis of main causes and risks related to genocide, war crimes and crimes against humanity, military intervention might be the wrong answer to crimes committed mainly by attrition. However, to the extent that attacks on camps and villages are considered the main risk for vulnerable groups, the inability to use military force has to be regarded a failure of the responsibility to protect.

3.1.2 Conclusions

Much has been said about the failure of early-warning and conflict prevention in the case of Darfur. Early on in the conflict, the United Nations missed multiple opportunities to act decisively on reports of large-scale violence and deter the government from continuing the pattern of attacks against civilians.[377] At that time, United Nations agencies on the ground had identified about 40 camps and villages that were main targets of Janjaweed and other attacks. It should have been considered possible to deploy a limited number of highly trained and self-sufficient troops to those locations in order to prevent further violence against civilians. The political space that would have been created through such a freeze could have been filled with many offers to the government and the rebels to arrive at an agreement. At that time, the use of airfields in Chad could have backed up such troops and implemented the existing no-fly zone over Darfur.[378] However, the main concern was the possible interruption of humanitarian delivery by the Government. While this would have raised serious concerns, it is important for the United Nations to be able to address the exceptional cases related to the responsibility to protect by setting priorities and taking risks based on a balance of rights and interests involved. It cannot be a serious argument that people cannot be saved from violence because the respective government might interrupt humanitarian deliveries to people in camps that are attacked or used as a means of genocide themselves.

The situation in Darfur offers an interesting challenge for the responsibility to protect. If the responsibility to protect was applied, response to the crisis would be more systematic as to the exhaustion of policy options, the documentation of manifest failure of the Government of Sudan to protect its own population and the need of physical protection of vulnerable groups through military means. Invoking the responsibility to protect would require the Secretariat to present and follow a clear line of argument as to the nature and consequences of the crimes committed, less as a legal classification but as a presentation of facts relevant for the establishment of the elements of crimes and manifest failure related to the responsibility to protect. The Secretary-General could recommend to the Security Council certain priority steps for the Government of Sudan to take with a view to prevent further violence, including indicators and timelines for its cooperation, similar to those developed by the Group of Experts of the Human Rights Council.[379]

Instead, in the absence of any political will to act, the Security Council passed numerous resolutions venturing into many different areas, including the establishment of an Independent International Commission on Inquiry (IICI), the referral of the situation in Sudan to the ICC, targeted sanctions and the demand to discontinue offensive military overflights. However, these measures did not follow any coherent strategy and did not include any serious follow-up that could focus discussions in the future. The lack of political determination among the Member States became obvious, when the Council conditioned the deployment of a Chapter VII peace operation explicitly on the consent of the Government of Sudan.

377 See e.g. *Sharat Srinivasan*, Minority Rights, Early Warning and Conflict Prevention: Lessons Learnt from Darfur, Minority Rights Group (2006).

378 See International Crisis Group, Getting the UN into Darfur, Africa Briefing N°43, 12 October 2006.

379 See e.g. *Rene Wadlow*, Darfur: The Responsibility to Protect, Newropeans Magazine, 2 April 2007.

Furthermore, notwithstanding the conclusions of the Srebrenica Report, the Security Council decided to deploy UNAMID without a peace to keep, as the Darfur Peace Agreement included only one faction of one rebel group and the mediation by the United Nations of political talks did not materialize, yet.[380]

At the same time, the situation in Darfur should be a clear case for the Security Council to apply the responsibility to protect based on its previous practice in cases of gross violations of human rights. With a view to the findings of the IICI on Darfur, it cannot be excluded that genocide is taking place in Darfur. The Commission found that the situation in 2005 fulfilled all elements of the definition of genocide with exception of the element of intent. The Commission also established that war crimes and crimes against humanity took place on a wide scale.[381]

The systematic approach of a continuum of steps could still be applied to the situation in Darfur, even though the situation is much more difficult and complex today than in 2004. In particular, robust protection of vulnerable groups from attacks could change significantly the cost-benefit ratio for the parties.[382]

3.2 Kenya

The post election crisis in Kenya at the beginning of 2008 has been considered by many a case of application of the responsibility to protect, including the Secretary-General, the Gareth Evans and Kofi Annan.[383] Therefore, it would be important to review United Nations action related to the situation in Kenya, limited to the responsibility to protect, in particular public statements and activities that could be related to the application of the concept.

3.2.1 United Nations action

In December 2007, the announcement of disputed election results lead to demonstrations and a wave of violence in the Rift Valley and other areas of western Kenya, which caused the death of 1,000 and the displacement of 300,000 civilians. While the violence was caused immediately by the political events, concerns mounted quickly that deep rooted ethnic tensions could escalate, when a circle of violence retribution put the Kikuyu against the Luo and Kalenjin ethnic groups. The

380 See U.N.-Doc S/RES/1769 (2007) of 31 July 2007, para. 1, 18.

381 Report of the International Commission of Inquiry on Darfur, U.N.-Doc. S/2005/60 of 1 February 2005.

382 See UN News Service, Joint UN-African Union mission in Darfur steps up presence at troubled camp, 3 September 2008.

383 Address by Mr. Kofi Annan on receiving the MacArthur Award for International Justice, New York, 20 March 2008.

logistic and operational support of the violence raised fear that the situation could escalate. Displaced persons often moved to areas, where their own ethnic group was in the majority.[384]

In his first public statement on the crisis, the Secretary-General expressed concern at the violence and called on the political leaders to resolve their differences peacefully.[385] With a view to the escalating violence, in a second statement, the Secretary-General reminded the Government as well as the political and religious leaders of Kenya of their legal and moral responsibility to protect the lives of innocent people, regardless of their racial religious or ethnic origin and urged them to prevent further violence.[386] While he did not repeat the direct reference to the responsibility to protect in his subsequent statements, the Secretary-General used related expressions, e.g. at the occasion of addressing the African Union Summit, he reminded political leaders in Kenya of their 'responsibility to do everything possible to resolve the source of the crisis peacefully.'[387]

International efforts had a difficult start, when the main political actors in Kenya basically rejected mediation by the United Nations or the AU.[388] Following different interventions, often on a personal basis, by different former heads of state and other African personalities, the parties finally agreed to a panel of three mediators, lead by former Secretary-General Kofi Annan. The panel acted on the invitation of President John Kofuor, Chairman of the AU, who had been rejected as mediator during his visit to Nairobi. The arrangement was mediated by The Elders, formed in July 2007 to use their unique collective skills to catalyze peaceful resolution to long-standing conflicts.[389] In their press release announcing the mediation, The Elders expressed their believe that it was essential for the government of Kenya to live up to its responsibility to protect civilians from mass atrocities and that the international community stood ready to help should the Kenyan government be unable to live up to that duty.[390]

On 1 February 2008, under the chairmanship of Kofi Annan, the parties agreed to an agenda for their dialogue, including immediate action to stop the violence, immediate measures to address the humanitarian crisis and promotion of reconciliation, steps to overcome the political crisis, and long-term issues and

384 See Kenya National Commission on Human Rights, On the brink of the precipice: A Human Rights Account of Kenya's Post-2007 Violence, August 2008.

385 Press Release SG/SM/11354, AFR/1639.

386 Press Release SG/SM/11356, AFR/1641.

387 Press Release SG/SM/11393, AFR/1651.

388 Kenya: Kufour Leaves As Talks Hit Stalemate, The Nation (Nairobi), 10 January 2008; Alistair Thomson, Analysis: Kenya failure bruises African Union Ambitions, Reuters Foundation, 11 January 2008. A slightly different account of events is given in: Kenya in Crisis, Crisis Group Africa Report Nr. 137, 21 February 2008, p. 21 et seq.

389 See for details: http://www.theelders.org/

390 The Elders, Elder Kofi Annan to lead African Union mediation panel in Kenya, 14 January 2008.

solutions.[391] While the first three agenda items were expected to be resolved immediately, the fourth item should be addressed over a period of one year until the end of January 2009.

The Secretary-General continued to express public support for the mediation and reiterated his deep concern at the protection of civilians and the respect for human rights in Kenya.[392] When negotiations of a final agreement arrived at difficulties during the final hours, he underlined that it was critical that the two main political leaders exercised their responsibility to the people of Kenya who continued to suffer amid a volatile situation.[393]

Other parts of the Secretariat took action with regard to the situation as well. The Department of Political Affairs supported the secretariat of the mediation panel by providing several staff members to assist with analysis, policy advice and general support. The High Commissioner for Human Rights dispatched a fact-finding mission to the country to look into the violence and allegations of grave human rights violations. The OHCHR mission also analyzed underlying civil, political, economic, social and cultural causes and formulated recommendations on possible accountability mechanisms. The report of the mission was made public in mid-March.[394] The Special Adviser on the Prevention of Genocide called for an immediate halt to the violence, noting that political and community leaders might be held accountable for their actions and urged them to meet their responsibility to protect the civilian population and prevent violence.

The Security Council considered the situation in Kenya under its agenda item entitled 'peace and security in Africa' and issued a Presidential Statement on 6 February 2008 expressing its concern at the killing, abuse and displacement of civilians.[395] The statement did not refer to the responsibility to protect. Even though the Member States requested the Secretary-General to be informed of the findings of the fact-finding missions by the High-Commissioner for Human Rights and the Special Adviser on the Prevention of Genocide, the situation in Kenya was not considered by the Council again. On 29 February 2008, the President read out a press statement welcoming the agreement that was finally reached by the parties.[396]

The agreement between the parties, Acting Together for Kenya: Agreement on the Principles of Partnership of the Coalition Government, states in its preamble the deep-seated and long-standing divisions which threatened the very existence of Kenya as a unified country. Even though the additional agreements include legal and constitutional reforms and a reconciliation commission to heal the wounds, the mediation concentrated on political power sharing rather than the root causes of the

391 Kenyan National Dialogue and Reconciliation, Annotated Agenda and Timetable, http://www. dialoguekenya.org/docs

392 Press Release SG/SM/11422, AFR/1658.

393 Press Release SG/SM/11438, AFR/1662.

394 United Nations Press Release, UN Human Rights Team Issues Report on Post-Election Violence in Kenya, 18 March 2008.

395 U.N.-Doc. S/PRST/2008/4 of 6 February 2008.

396 Press Release SC/9265-AFR/1664.

violence.[397] So far, the parties limited their activities on the fourth agenda item of the National Dialogue to political declarations and the reconfirmation of agreed principles.[398]

3.2.2 Conclusions

The involvement of the United Nations in the post election crisis in Kenya raises a number of concerns regarding the application of the responsibility to protect.

The international community did not act through the United Nations, but rather an NGO that gained access to the country where the United Nations and the African Union had failed. The Security Council, the Secretariat and the funds and agencies involved in the crisis in Kenya did not follow an integrated approach in response to a common assessment of a risk of genocide, war crimes and crimes against humanity. In fact, the report of the OHCHR fact-finding mission only mentioned that violence was perpetrated largely along ethnic lines. The recommendations mainly supported the ongoing activities of the mediation rather than proposing specific measures that the Government of Kenya must take in order to prevent genocide and crimes against humanity. The report of the Special Adviser on the Prevention of Genocide was not made public or shared widely within the United Nations agencies, funds and departments. Consequently, no common analysis or assessment exists as well for current United Nations support to Kenya in meeting its responsibility to rebuild and prevent large-scale violence based on ethnicity after general elections as experienced already in 1992 and 1994 as well as after the referendum on the constitution in 2005.

In addition, the mediation did not propose a continuum of steps which the Government of Kenya should take in order to prevent further violence. Only a political settlement that restored legitimacy and state authority could offer a viable end to the crisis, as long as violence was perceived as the only option for resolving the electoral dispute and longstanding grievances.[399] Nevertheless, there was no list of measures included in the agreements to mitigate a perceived risk of genocide or crimes against humanity being committed.

Finally, there was no visible preparedness by the United Nations to implement a continuum of steps, including coercive measures, should the Government of Kenya manifestly fail to meet its responsibility to protect. The United Nations were not prepared for any emergency to protect people physically against further attacks.

Therefore, the discussion of Kenya as precedent for the application of the responsibility to protect might be motivated more by the wish to present a case,

397 Agreement on the Principles of Partnership of the Coalition Government, http://www.dialoguekenya.org/agreements.aspx

398 Statement of Principles on Long-term issues and solutions from 23 May updated with implementation matrix, http://www.dialoguekenya.org/agreements.aspx

399 International Crisis Group, FN. 388, p. 21.

where no military intervention took place, than by any particular methodology applied during the crisis.

3.3 Myanmar

On 3 and 4 May 2008, cyclone Nargis caused a 12-food storm surge that submerged under water large parts of the Irrawaddy Delta region of Myanmar. According to a report compiled by the United Nations, the Myanmar government and the Association of East Asian Nations, based on a detailed survey of affected villages in June, about 85,000 people died and 54,000 are still missing. The storm destroyed 450,000 houses and damaged 350,000; more than 4,000 schools and 75 % of local health facilities were wrecked. In addition, in the primarily seaside and agricultural area, people lost their livelihoods, when livestock was killed and tools, equipment and seeds swept away.[400]

Despite the emerging scale of the disaster, during the days following the storm the Government of Myanmar allowed little aid to enter the country, restricted the movement of humanitarian workers in the delta and did not issue visa to additional international aid workers waiting in Bangkok to enter the country.

In response to the position of the Government of Myanmar, French Foreign Minister Bernard Kouchner, suggested that the United Nations invoked the responsibility to protect as a basis for a Security Council resolution that should allow delivery of international aid without the government's permission. He suggested that the French, British and US navy presence on standby should get involved based on an authorization by the Council.[401]

While the suggestion was not taken up by the Security Council, it provoked different statements related to the applicability of the responsibility to protect on the situation in Myanmar. Under-Secretary-General for Humanitarian Affairs, John Holmes, rejected the idea on the basis of practicability. Without sufficient people on the ground to secure distribution of aid to all vulnerable, air drops or other military activities would not improve the situation.[402] Gareth Evans cautioned to extend the application of the responsibility to protect on any emergency situations that caused life-threatening risks to a high number of people. He recalled that the responsibility to protect has been developed in order to address exceptional situations similar to Rwanda, Srebrenica, Kosovo or Somalia. Only if the denial of aid or access to life-saving resources constituted a way of committing crimes against humanity or

400 Post-Nargis Joint Assessment. A report prepared by the Tripartite Core Group comprised of Representatives of the Government of the Union of Myanmar, the Association of Southeast Asian Nations and the United Nations with the support of the Humanitarian and Development Community, July 2008.

401 France urges UN to force cyclone aid on Myanmar, International Herald Tribune, 7 May 2008.

402 Myanmar Faces Pressure to Allow Major Aid Effort, New York Times, 8 May 2008.

genocide, the application could be considered.[403] Edward Luck expressed similar concerns.[404]

It can be concluded that the debate on the application of the responsibility to protect initiated a useful discussion on the limits and origins of the concept. At the same time, the relationship between humanitarian access, humanitarian principles and the responsibility to protect has not been addressed fundamentally. Concerns remain that the concepts could weaken rather than support each other.

4. *The way forward*

The discussion about operationalizing the responsibility to protect has to be seen in the wider context of the reform of the United Nations. Full implementation of the responsibility to protect by the United Nations may require reforming fundamental components of the organization, including membership and veto power in the Security Council.[405] In addition, consensus on the interpretation of sovereignty, the right to intervene in situations of gross human rights violations against the will of the government concerned or criteria for the application of military action will be difficult to pursue in abstract. At the same time, the responsibility to protect can create new dynamics for reform challenges that could not be met at the World Summit, such as a limitation of the veto or the establishment of a standing military capacity. In any case, the Secretary-General can initiate immediate steps towards the operationalization of the concept without prior consent among Member States on all its elements, i.e. based on a common minimum denominator. Rather than exchanging, once again, well-known principled positions, the meeting of the General Assembly on the responsibility to protect expected for the beginning of 2009 provides an opportunity to initiate discussions of limited steps for a limited number of extreme cases. While a case-by-case approach is not preferable over an approach on a principled basis, the ultimate aim of any activities towards the operationalization of the responsibility to protect is the protection of people against the most serious violations of their fundamental human rights. In this regard, the term ethnic cleansing among the listed crimes allows a more factual than legal assessment of events on the ground that should be explored more systematically for its capacity to provide an entry point for the application of the responsibility to protect.[406]

403 Gareth Evans, Facing up to our responsibilities, The Guardian, 12 May 2008.

404 Im Gespräch Edward C. Luck, UN-Sonderberater, Sollen wir einen Krieg ins Zyklon-Gebiet tragen?, Frankfurter Allgemeine Zeitung, 15 May 2008.

405 *Hugh Beach*, Just War and the Responsibility to Protect: Developments in UN Peacekeeping and Humanitarian Intervention, Disarmament Diplomacy, Issue No. 80, 2005.

406 *Evans*, FN. 52, p. 12 et seq.

The following considerations assume that the Secretary-General can make decisions for the Secretariat, funds and agencies to develop a work-plan for United Nations action towards the operationalization of the responsibility to protect before consensus on the interpretation of all details of the Outcome Document can be secured. While the proposal aims at providing a framework for the main elements of such an approach, it should be read in conjunction with the observations in the previous chapters.[407]

Unfortunately, the recent experience in Darfur, Somalia and other cases of alleged genocide, war crimes and crimes against humanity confirms the assessment of the Independent Inquiry on Rwanda that the United Nations has failed to act for lack of resources and lack of political commitment.[408] Under the leadership of the Secretary-General, these two gaps have to be addressed.

4.1 Leadership opportunities for the Secretary-General

The Summit Outcome document stressed the need for the General Assembly to continue consideration of the responsibility to protect.[409] This provision has been interpreted as a general caveat that, to some extent, limited the agreement expressed in the other parts of this section.[410]

At the same time, according to article 99 of the Charter, the Secretary-General is entitled to take political initiative in the maintenance of international peace and security. This provision is considered to form the legal basis for every political activity of the Secretary-General, which he performs on his own initiative.[411] The right to initiative of the Secretary-General covers 'any matter', while the right of Member States is limited to 'any dispute or situation'.

The application of the right to initiative by different Secretaries-General offers only limited precedent for the implementation of the responsibility to protect. In 1971, without reference to article 99, U Thant circulated a memorandum on the developments in East Pakistan and the possible consequences for international peace and security. In the application of Perez de Cuellar, the right to initiative gained new substance in including concrete recommendations for Security Council action to ensure the maintenance of international peace and security. Thus, it can be assumed that, ultimately, it would be for the Secretary-General to call on the Security Council to take action in cases of genocide, war crimes and crimes against humanity, similar to the letter by Boutros-Ghali of 29 April 1994 in the case of Rwanda.[412]

407 See for a detailed list of the challenges for the United Nations e.g. *Marc Saxer*, The Responsibility to Protect, FES Briefing Paper 2, April 2008; *von Schorlemer*, FN. 47.

408 Rwanda report, FN. 259, p. 3.

409 Summit Outcome, para. 139.

410 *Stahn*, FN. 17, p. 105.

411 Fiedler, Article 99, in: *Simma*, FN. 97, para. 5.

412 U.N.-Doc. S/1994/518 of 29 April 1994.

More importantly, article 99 of the Charter provides the legal basis for leadership of the Secretary-General on the operationalization of the responsibility to protect within the Secretariat, agencies and funds. The provision has been interpreted earlier as requiring the Secretary-General to collect and evaluate a broad range of information. With regard to the prevention of genocide, war crimes and crimes against humanity, the Security Council requested the Secretary-General to bring to its attention cases of serious violations of international law, including human rights and humanitarian law and on potential conflicts arising from ethnic or religious conflicts.[413] It has been concluded earlier that, on this basis, the Secretary-General is entitled to develop the necessary methodologies and resources in order to fulfill this task.

In an attempt to exercise leadership, the Secretary-General requested the Special Adviser, who works primarily on the responsibility to protect, to develop the conceptual, institutional and political dimensions of the responsibility to protect consistent with points agreed in paragraphs 138 and 139 of the Outcome document.[414]

The interpretation of the Outcome document to introduce 'three pillars' of the responsibility to protect, however, risks to lose the continuum of measures that, according to their public statements, the Member States appeared to have accepted as an important element of the concept.[415]

The Secretary-General followed a phased approach to developing a joint office with the Special Adviser on the Prevention of Genocide, who had a distinct, but closely related mandate. The joint office is expected to encourage operational departments, funds and agencies to incorporate the responsibility to protect and genocide prevention into their existing activities and reporting procedures. In addition, an inter-departmental and inter-agency Committee should be established in order to meet every month and as required in crisis situations for the considerations of case-specific or generic recommendations on issues related to the responsibility to protect. During the first phase, the existing posts of the Special Adviser on the Prevention of Genocide would be reallocated to tasks related to the work of the joint office. Once the General Assembly had the opportunity to review the Secretary-General's report on the responsibility to protect, presumably in early 2009, it could be in a better position to consider further resource allocations.[416]

An administrative structure is an important requirement to allocate resources to implement any strategy for the operationalization of the responsibility to protect. Too often, however, the establishment of new structures such as Working Groups or Secretariat offices remains the only element of a United Nations strategy. The

413 U.N.-doc. S/RES/1366 (2001) of 30 August 2001.

414 Letter of the Secretary-General addressed to the President of the Security Council, U.N.-Doc. S/2007/721 of 7 December 2007.

415 See above A.3.1.

416 For reflections on the way ahead see Edward C. Luck, The United Nations and the Responsibility to Protect, in: *The Stanley Foundation* (ed.), Policy Analysis Brief, August 2008.

operationalization of the responsibility to protect seems to require activities within four broad areas: (1) consultations with Member States to establish the common minimum denominator, (2) consultations with departments, agencies and funds to develop the repertoire of measures short of military intervention, (3) monitoring the approximately ten country situations which might qualify for the application of the responsibility to protect with a view to establish capacities and needs, and (4) consultations with DPKO and Member States on ways to establish military capacities for operations in situations of imminent or ongoing genocide, war crimes and crimes against humanity limited to the physical protection of groups at risk.

The history of the responsibility to protect and its current interpretation does not provide for distinguishing situations relevant for its application from other conflicts and emergencies other than by the gravity of the crimes that have been committed. A list of criteria for the application of the responsibility to protect has not been developed and agreed upon. The ECPS, the Policy Committee and Integrated Task Forces can provide the necessary resources and expertise to address a deteriorating situation through a system-wide approach. An additional structure should address the temporary challenges of the operationalization of the responsibility to protect listed under (1) and (2) above, while fact-finding, analysis, early warning and other measures should be left to the existing framework under the leadership of the Special Adviser on the Prevention of Genocide. Mainstreaming of the responsibility to protect is supported best by using existing mechanisms of inter-departmental and inter-agency cooperation, which would be adequate for the task of developing joint country strategies.

4.2 Closing the commitment gap

It can be assumed that increased political commitment of Member States would result in providing the United Nations with the required resources.[417] Governments or coalitions of States have agreed in the past to carry out operations with United Nations authorization in situations of ongoing genocide, war crimes and crimes against humanity if very strong national interests were at stake. It appears from past experience that outside intervention will not be an option until Western powers in particular feel threatened by a conflict.[418] The main political challenge for governments is the acceptance by its national population of casualties vis-à-vis national interests in the mandate. Often, Member States have not been clear in defining their national interests in taking such risks. The responsibility to protect could provide a valuable framework to define national interests, prioritize foreign policy goals and mobilize political support.

417 After World War II, $ 1,448 million had been invested in the reconstruction of Germany through the Marshall Plan between 1948 and 1951. It is estimated that the US-led war in Iraq costs $ 12 billion per month.

418 *Evans*, FN. 52, p. 17 et seq.

The main interest-based arguments provided for collective action by the United Nations in cases of mass atrocities include the concern that lack of unity within the Security Council regarding a country situation could weaken its decision-making in other, unrelated, situations as well. Non-intervention in cases of mass atrocities could also weaken the global authority of the United Nations and motivate Member States to take unilateral action outside the Security Council. Furthermore, it could also encourage other governments to follow the same approach in the absence of United Nations action. The failure to protect the people of Rwanda has had a negative impact on their relationship with the United Nations, which also caused a limitation of United Nations influence on the situation in the sub-region. Ultimately, it is argued that experience has shown that behavior against international standards, in the long term, undermines the national interests of the State itself as its international influence diminishes and outside intervention becomes more likely.

The collective failure of the United Nations to react adequately to prevent genocide in Rwanda and Srebrenica and, most recently, in Darfur, has shown that interest-based foreign policy does not lead automatically to results in conformity with the Charter and the history of the organization. The challenge is to convince governments to define more long-term global interests in collective action against genocide, war crimes and crimes against humanity instead of short-term national goals.

The discussion in the Security Council, whether genocide was taking place in Darfur or Rwanda, which replaced the discussion about timely and decisive action, indicated that Member States no longer share a common ethic consensus on the basis of which they could rally behind collective action to halt or prevent mass atrocities under all circumstances. While Kofi Annan repeatedly appealed to the Security Council for action to halt violence in Darfur, apparently, he did not provide reasons compelling enough for Member States to act. It is difficult to imagine how, in the long-term, the United Nations can retain its role in development and peacekeeping without basic common values of the Member States. The responsibility to protect offers the opportunity as much as it depends on a common ethic position shared among all Member States, notwithstanding ideologies currently exacerbated by the 'war on terror', preemptive military action, neo-colonialism, cultural relativism, 'clash of civilizations' or religious fundamentalism.

Discussions among Member States in the General Assembly and in the Human Rights Council reflect a general trend of gradual withdrawal from international standards on human rights, democracy and the rule of law offering exceptional security or economic circumstances as justification. It has become increasingly difficult to agree on joint action in support of human rights and justice in extreme cases, overriding national sovereignty.[419]

419 See for a detailed analysis from the perspective of the European Union *Richard Gowan/ Franziska Brantner*, A Global Force for Human Rights? An Audit of European Power at the UN, European Council on Foreign Relations, 2008.

In his speech in Berlin in July 2008, the Secretary-General referred to the ideas, ideals and aspirations on which the United Nations was built. He reminded his audience that the people of the world were inspired by the United Nations, because it tried to accomplish the impossible. The responsibility to protect stood for the most noble and enduring in the human condition.[420]

While these references are important in the context of the responsibility to protect, the leadership of the Secretary-General will be required in a deeper sense. Based on the principles of the United Nations and the history of the Charter, he will have to represent the underlying 'final justification' for the legitimacy of collective action in certain country situations. Only on this basis, the Secretary-General could hope to trigger a change in the discussion from national interests to collective aspirations. With a view to his South-Korean origin, Ban Ki-moon could make a historic contribution to the United Nations by leading the discussion and preserving important principles in new circumstances.[421] Similar to a national constitution, the principles of the Charter will prevail only if Member States share common ethic positions as a basis for its interpretation. This would not require the development of a comprehensive United Nations ethics, but some basic rules deriving from the world's main religions and philosophies.

According to their own accounts, the Permanent Representatives of Slovenia and Bangladesh respectively referred to universal values when leading negotiations on the responsibility to protect on behalf of the President of the General Assembly during the preparations of the World Summit 2005. As discussed in a broader context, including the universality of human rights, the common ethic consensus within the United Nations on the responsibility to protect requires the agreement on a minimum of values, positions and measures.[422] Further indicators derive from the acceptance of the ‚just-war' theory by the major world religions and philosophies.[423] This global ethos should not replace existing religions or cultures, but define the necessary common minimum of values and objectives in realizing the common global interests. A United Nations ethos has to be accepted in its main elements by different religions as well as agnostics or atheists. This global ethos required for the implementation of the responsibility to protect will not be a total consensus, but a necessary minimum deriving from the global connection of people around the world through existing or perceived links created by war, conflict and mass atrocities. It becomes clear from the reaction in the different countries to these events that a global consensus in the understanding of truth and justice exists independent of a consensus on the different philosophical theories about their respective content. In 2007, the Chicago Council on Global Affairs reported that the majority of people polled in 12 countries agreed that the Security Council had the responsibility to

420 Press Release SG/SM/11701.

421 See on the influence of Dag Hammarskjöld's political ethic on the United Nations *Manuel Fröhlich*, Political Ethics and the United Nations. Dag Hammarskjöld as Secretary-General, London, 2008, p. 183 et seq.

422 See for the following *Hans Küng*, Projekt Weltethos, München, 1990.

423 See for detailed references *Evans*, FN. 52, p. 140.

authorize the use of military force to protect people from severe human rights violations even if this meant acting against the will of their own government. The Chinese public showed the highest level of support with 76 %, followed by the United States with 74 %, the Palestinian territories with 69 % and Israel 64 %.[424] This elementary consensus is often hidden behind discussions on fundamental questions in the context of existing human rights obligations, where culture and religion plays a dominant role. However, the limited core consensus is not less, but an essential part of the agreement on human rights and reactions should avoid to argue in terms of 'undermining' or 'falling back' when such differences occur. Recalling the fundamental agreement underlying the discussion might be supportive rather than detrimental. Furthermore, moral consensus does not exist in abstract, but with regard to particular circumstances and situations. At the same time, it is not static, but moves over time from more general to more precise obligations and vice versa depending on the situation at hand.

Respect for human rights and humanitarian law as such cannot be the only content of a global ethos on the responsibility to protect as the consensus to protect people from genocide, war crimes and crimes against humanity pre-date human rights codifications. The common consensus is not a repetition of existing human rights obligations or an agreement on positions in controversial areas of political debate, e.g. the right to intervene or limitations to use one's veto. Instead, the consensus is the underlying minimum position that will allow different religions and cultures to move forward in a particular situation. This approach reflects the reality of different cultures, religions and societies that do not exist as monolithic blocks, but are fluent in their borders and must seek common solutions.

Research on the values and convictions of different religions revealed two concrete elements of an ethical consensus that are directly relevant for the responsibility to protect (1) human beings must be treated humanely, (2) do to others what you want to be done to yourself. The Declaration of the Parliament of the world religions[425] agreed on four principles based on this consensus: (a) culture of peace and respect for life (b) solidarity and a fair economic order (c) tolerance and mutual respect, including truthfulness (d) culture of non-discrimination and equality, including between men and women. All of these principles can be found in the preamble and opening articles of the United Nations Charter. The ethical minimum is, thus, well reflected in the very foundation of the organization that the Secretary-General should preserve. Moving forward on this basis to express the requirements of the implementation of the responsibility to protect provide the Secretary-General with firm ground beyond the ongoing discussions on culture, religions etc. In this regard, the responsibility to protect is not primarily a further development of legal

424 Available at http://www.thechicagocouncil.org/publication_report_list.php?report_type=P#POShttp://www.thechicagocouncil.org/UserFiles/File/POS_Topline%20Reports/POS %202007_R2P/2007%20Genocide_report.pdf

425 Declaration Toward a Global Ethic, Parliament of the World's Religions, Chicago, 4 September 1993.

standards or of the operational capacity of the United Nations, but the expression of a consensus that pre-dated the Charter.

In order to fill the commitment gap, the United Nations require an ethically determined vision for its role in cases of genocide, war crimes and crimes against humanity, and concrete concepts for its implementation. The development of such concepts requires a clear separation from national interests as well as the idealism of human rights and peace for all. The ethical vision must be result oriented and conscious of its possible negative impact. It is important to recall that common standards of behavior derive from the practical needs of the governments concerned. International provisions of human rights and humanitarian law neither developed on their own nor claimed a peaceful and ideal world, but came into being and prevailed for the reason that they follow the facts and circumstances and say what should be. The level of ethical agreement on those basic rules cannot be determined by the level of breach of its obligations.

For the Secretary-General, the description of the consensus should avoid technical or legal language as well as transporting certain cultural determinations that might be unacceptable for some cultures. The drafting history of the Outcome Document, the ICISS and other reports showed that the three crimes have not been used mainly within their technical and legal limitations, but as a description of situations that are so 'conscious-shocking' for Member States to lead to collective action based on a consensus that such crimes must be halted. Therefore, the discussion of the Secretary-General should avoid technical aspects, which should be dealt with on an academic and working level, but concentrate on the elements of an ethical consensus that could form the basis for a decision on a continuum of steps in a concrete situation. The process addressing racial discrimination or the development of the rule of law related activities could offer positive examples for formulating common positions beyond different cultures and religions.[426] In this understanding, ethic means responsibility rather than idealism. The Secretary-General could promote such an ethic by calling on Member States to be more transparent on the implementation of their obligations to prevent genocide, war crimes and crimes against humanity at the national level in concrete situations as well as applying these standards consequently within his own responsibility.[427] Furthermore, following a proposal by the Special Adviser on the Prevention of Genocide in 2005, the Secretary-General could encourage the appointment of focal points in national governments with a view to address directly questions related to the prevention of genocide.

While exercising leadership with a view to Member States, the ethic consensus would provide also orientation to the United Nations Secretariat, in particular OCHA, OHCHR and the Office of Legal Affairs (OLA) for the development of

426 See e.g. *Michael Banton*, International Action Against Racial Discrimination, Oxford, 1996.

427 See e.g. Martise Simons, Belgium Jury Convicts 4 of 1994 War Crimes in Rwanda, New York Times, 9 June 2001; Colum Lynch, Rwandan to Retain Darfur Peacekeeping Post, Washington Post, 2 October 2008.

indicators for the exceptional character of relevant situations that would form the basis of an early-warning system, civilian capacities, military capacities and other elements within the Secretariat. The Secretariat would need to assess which measures were available to the United Nations to implement human rights and humanitarian law in a situation of imminent or ongoing mass atrocities. If the United Nations just continued normal activities related to monitoring, assistance and capacity building, in the face of genocide, war crimes and crimes against humanity, it would contribute to the weakening of obligations deriving from the global ethos. The United Nations message to Member States where mass atrocities are ongoing or imminent must be the same from the humanitarian, economic or political parts of the system. At the same time, that message will only be convincing if it is based on the global ethos and applies the same standard equally to all countries and situations.

The application of the responsibility to protect requires decisions on its relationship to mandates of the organization in related areas such as humanitarian aid, human rights and rule of law.

The current discourse on the protection of civilians in armed conflict remains focused on the humanitarian access and the protection of humanitarian workers. This discourse is too wide and too narrow at the same time.[428] The implementation of the responsibility to protect requires a clear concept for legitimate multinational intervention to end gross human rights violations by both governments and non-governmental actors. Therefore, the term of 'civilian population' should be avoided in the context of the responsibility to protect and replaced by 'peoples at risk'. The United Nations need to develop appropriate measures for a humanitarian response in the exceptional cases covered by the responsibility to protect.

The human rights policy of the United Nations will only be effective if it supports, not undermines, the obligations of Member States in difficult circumstances. In this regard, it would be required to define priorities of human rights obligations in cases of imminent or ongoing genocide, war crimes and crimes against humanity, while retaining the principle of inalienability and indivisibility. Fundamental rights of the person, in particular the right to life, personal liberty, not to be tortured, not to be arbitrarily arrested or discriminated against on the basis of being part of a vulnerable group, should be prioritized over other political, economic and social rights. As shown above, these rights reflect less of a perceived Western model, but obligations valid under all circumstances and deriving from all religions and cultures. A joint approach could be deduced from the different claims of legality and morality that governments quote to excuse their violations of law and morale. These priorities, in turn, would inform the definition of a continuum of steps the government should take in order to meet its responsibility to protect, including coercive measures.

The mobilization of political will should focus on the international community as much as the government and other alleged perpetrators concerned. With regard to the latter, research and analysis on violence against civilians should be taken into

428 See above B.2.1.2.

consideration. According to such findings, in most cases, anti-civilian violence is deliberate, i.e. it is agreed, pre-planned and carried out as ordered. Nevertheless, the international community prefers to address such situations with the reference to legal obligations and moral norms deriving from international human rights and humanitarian law. These references are important to establish accountability, but they fail to expose the political purpose or thinking behind such activities. At least in the context of the responsibility to protect, civilian suffering cannot be considered inevitable consequences of conflict. The crimes are committed for a particular political purpose as part of the strategy of war. Some research distinguishes types of civilian suffering, including massacres, rape and sexual violence, impoverishment, making the enemy hungry and ill, emotional suffering, and post-war suffering. These pattern of suffering are committed based on underlying political considerations which can range from genocidal ideologies, through exceptional arguments to the acceptance of mere coincidence or tragic. In the experience of the United Nations the lack of exposing such underlying political considerations in discussions on the situation often leads to a perpetuating discourse on false perceptions. Ultimately, violations against civilians are a means of winning a war. In countering such a policy, the United Nations must be able to deter, inhibit and dissuade perpetrators and attract pro-civilian conduct.[429] At least in situations, where the responsibility to protect would be applicable, the discourse between the United Nations and the respective Government should be changed accordingly.

Measures short of intervention are often not taken by the Security Council as Member States consider the situation from the back end.[430] A decision on sanctions or investigative measures are taken within a broader consideration of national interests in the respective country and the likelihood of any sanctions having to be implemented by force later on in the conflict. Thus, political commitment to act will depend often on the availability of acceptable options. In this regard, it is important to develop a list of measures that could be proposed to different organs of the United Nations with a view to defining the continuum of steps which lies at the heart of the responsibility to protect. In this regard, it is important to include steps on the implementation of the responsibility to rebuild, when presenting the continuum. The consideration of military intervention as ‚ultimate measure' often leads to leaving the continuum incomplete. Over time, preventive measures can be move from the short-term to the mid- and long-term based on causal links established through experience in country situations rather than general considerations on the relationship between security, development and human rights.[431] In this context, the preoccupation of the Security Council with the separation of operations under Chapter VI and VII appears artificial and with limited practical relevance. As

429 See e.g. *Slim/ Mancini-Griffoli*, FN. 250.

430 Similarly *Evans*, FN. 52, p. 84 et seq.

431 The example of hate-speech is a case in point. After the ICTR had established the causal link between the activities of Radio Milles Collines and the subsequent genocide, government accepted hate-speech as an early-warning indicator for genocide. See Nahamana, Barayagwiz and Ngeze, Case No. ICTR-99-52-T.

discussions about UNAMID revealed, both operations require the consent of the receiving government unless the Member States are ready to force their way into the country.

A provisional review of the application of such measures in previous cases of genocide, war crimes and crimes against humanity suggests that in order to be successful any consensual measure requires that the negative consequences for the Member State of non-compliance are higher than the expected positive impact of a continuation of previous behavior. Different factors can influence this balance, including the position of peer states, individual consequences stemming e.g. from targeted sanctions or arrest warrants, or unity within the Council that further measures would be taken in case of non-compliance. The common ethos could provide powerful support for creating the necessary imbalance for Member States to change their approach.

Ultimately, in the face of a list of practical measures based on a global ethos, it will be more difficult to dismiss the responsibility to protect as a neo-colonialist concept, riddled with inconsistencies and driven by selfish motives on the part of the developed nations. Fragile states will be more exposed seeing themselves as possible targets and suspicious of the emphasis laid on abuses of human rights, which they fear, could be applied to their own records.

4.3 Closing the resource gap

It has been acknowledged that the United Nations will not be able to respond to all conflicts around the world. In this regard, the responsibility to protect provides a framework to define priorities and prevent, to some extent, the perception of double-standard, when defining situations that require the attention of the Security Council for their potential threat to international peace and security.

Early-warning and the responsibility to prevent genocide, war crimes and crimes against humanity will require cooperation of different mandates, institutions and organs within the United Nations. Notwithstanding the legendary experience of the Special Rapporteur of the Commission on Human Rights on extrajudicial, summary and arbitrary executions, who reported upon his return from a mission to Rwanda on his concerns that genocide might take place[432], the Security Council did not establish a regular exchange with relevant Special Rapporteurs or the High Commissioner for Human Rights on situations of concern. Instead, Member States insisted on deleting references to Human Rights Council resolutions in draft Security Council resolutions claiming conflict of mandates with the General Assembly.[433] It would be required to remind the Council on a regular basis of rule 39 of its Rules of Procedure, i.e. the possibility to invite members of the Secretariat or other persons to

432 Report by Mr. B.W. Ndiaye. Special Rapporteur, on his mission to Rwanda from 8 to 17 April 1993, U.N.-Doc. E/CN.4/1994/7/Add.1 of 11 August 1993.

433 See above B.2.2.3.

supply it with information or assistance, as well as the content of relevant resolutions related to particular country situations, such as Somalia and Iraq. In resolution 1296 (2000) the Security Council found that targeting civilians in armed conflict and the denial of humanitarian access to civilian populations afflicted by war may themselves constitute threats to international peace and security.[434]

While the benefits of prevention and early-intervention has been argued repeatedly and from different viewpoints, including the economic costs involved in post-conflict peace building, efforts of the United Nations remain scattered around the organization with limited interrelations. The responsibility to prevent could provide a framework for the different initiatives by bringing them behind a common cause, preferably under the leadership of the Special Adviser on the Prevention of Genocide. Agreements on methodology and analysis could influence positively further cooperation in the area of conflict prevention. As an ultima ratio for United Nations action, it could also provide a framework for other areas of work and provide orientation for setting priorities.

The responsibility to react will require an additional military concept for United Nations operations as its primary aim will be the physical protection to stop the killing of civilians. The discussion of military intervention as ultima ratio within the responsibility to react is mainly referring to cases in the past equated with humanitarian intervention.[435] In these cases Member states opposed intervention, because of the consequences for the government and the political system of the State concerned.[436] Limited interventions to protect vulnerable groups at places of possible attacks were much more acceptable and, regarding the specific protection from genocide, war crimes and crimes against humanity, not less effective. However, they required the acceptance that a multinational military intervention in such situations will not address the root causes of the conflict and might jeopardize temporarily the humanitarian access to the victims.[437] It might as well influence the military balance within a conflict that delivers a decisive military victory to one party. However, in circumstances where genocide, war crimes and crimes against humanity take place, any development which stops the fighting and brings the parties to the negotiation table is preferable to the status quo. The impartiality of the United Nations is based on the Charter, which includes a number of values and historic experience. Equal treatment of all parties irrespective of their characteristics as perpetrators and victims damaged the credibility of the United Nations in the past.[438] It is the task of the Secretary-General to uphold the Charter and represent the interests of the organization. It is important for the Secretary-General to ensure that

434 U.N.-Doc. S/RES/1296 (2000) of 19 April 2000.

435 See Gareth Evans, Operationalizing R2P in Coercive Peace Operations, Presentation to Working Group on Peace Operations and the Protection of Civilians, San Remo, 5 September 2008 available at http://www.crisisgroup.org/home/index.cfm?id=4521&l=1.

436 See above C 1.2.2.2.

437 Report of the Secretary-General on protection for humanitarian assistance to refugees and others in conflict situation, U.N.-Doc. S/1998/883 of 22 September 1998, para. 24 et seq.

438 Brahimi report, FN. 240, p. ix.

when the United Nations sends forces, they are prepared to confront war and violence with the ability and the determination to defeat the perpetrators. At the same time, it should be understood that force alone cannot create peace, but the space in which peace may be built.[439]

Based on the priorities deriving from the common ethic position, the Secretary-General could provide clarification on the activities expected from intervening forces. Based on the experience in Bunia, Rwanda and Sierra Leone these activities would be limited in time and scope. The United Nations would require highly trained and readily equipped troops. General Romeo Dallaire argued that 5,000 troops and some additional measures, such as the jamming of radio frequencies, could have halted the slaughter in Rwanda at an early stage.[440] With a view to the exceptional character of the situations considered in the context of the responsibility to protect and the difficulties of the Member States to contribute the troops required for UNAMID and other ongoing missions, a military concept for the implementation of the responsibility to protect could revive discussions on an international emergency force.[441] Furthermore, direct United Nations command could ease concerns of Member States that interventions of regional or Western powers could be authorized by the Security Council under the pretext of the responsibility to protect.[442]

In the absence of such a contingent, training of peacekeepers could address the challenges for the military related to the protection of civilians from genocide, war crimes and crimes against humanity. National training centers could make an important contribution to the discussion on the international level as well, if they included the responsibility to protect in their training as they included e.g. sexual exploitation. In this regard, it is important that the military and the training centers cooperate across borders on the review and development of measures of direct prevention and reaction to ongoing or imminent large-scale violence.[443] However, ultimately, it remains the responsibility of the Member States to train and equip their own forces according to the mandate they give to them. So far, Member States did not work on the development of measures to intervene in internal conflict situations involving the crimes listed in the Outcome document.

The experience from situations and in the past has shown that conflict situations cannot be distinguished neatly in responsibility to protect cases and others. Rather, the development of conflicts is dynamic and genocide, war crimes and crimes

439 Op. cit., p. viii.

440 See for details *Romeo Dallaire*, Shake Hands with the Devil: The Failure of Humanity in Rwanda, Canada, 2003. His assessment was confirmed by *Scott Feil*, Preventing Genocide: How the Early Use of Force Might Have Succeeded in Rwanda, Report to the Carnegie Commission on Preventing Deadly Conflict, April 1998.

441 See recently *Morton Abramovitz/ Thomas Pickering*, Making intervention work, Foreign Affairs, Vol. 87 (2008), No. 5, p. 100 et seq.

442 *Holt*, FN. 300, p. 15 et seq.

443 *Emma Birikorang*, Operationalizing the “Responsibility to Protect”, available at http://www.apsta-africa.org/news/article02032007.php

against humanity could occur after a situation is already pending at the Security Council. There needs to be agreement and buy-in by all concerned that applying the responsibility to protect is a useful strategy in a particular case. Only then the case will move forward and a strategy for the whole United Nations is required that distributes tasks and roles and develops a time-table for action. In the exceptional circumstances where it applies, the responsibility to protect would lose its added value if it was introduced through the back door in order not to undermine humanitarian access, political negotiations or a peace process. Based on a universal ethic as expressed in the Charter, the responsibility to protect offers an opportunity for strategic joint action under the clear determination to use force, when required and engage in reconstruction. This is a different task from identifying risk situations as such and calls for different skills and experience. With regard to information analysis and the consideration of risks of genocide and other large scale violations, the earlier proposal of a body related to ECPS would be preferable to a self-standing entity.[444]

With a view to this scenario, the Secretariat could develop a more forward looking approach regarding the responsibility to protect. With a view to the exceptional character of the situations and the general agreement that this exception would be applicable to about ten current conflict situations, the Special Adviser on the Prevention of Genocide and the Special Adviser, dealing mainly with the responsibility to protect, should lead efforts within the Secretariat to prepare a continuum of steps and the analysis of influential factors involved in each situation. The practical application of the elements proposed here does not require prior agreement of Member States or the Security Council.

The ultimate step of military intervention will occur only after other measures have been exhausted and as part of a continuum of steps, including the responsibility to rebuild. Robust military intervention could be authorized by the Security Council for a Member State, a coalition of Member States, a regional organization or a peacekeeping operation already present on the ground. The assessment of available military resources should include a consideration whether physical protection is indeed possible within the context of contemporary peace operations. The review of the contribution by previous peace operations to prevent or halt gross human rights violations seems to suggest that the question must be answered negative.[445] At the same time, national military doctrine as well as NATO standards provide for operations in areas where widespread human rights violations, ethnic cleansing and genocide are committed and include action related to the physical protection of potential victims.[446] However, these provisions do not indicate how exactly these tasks should be undertaken. The Brahimi report found that any peace operation of the United Nations must be able to pose a credible deterrent threat to potential

444 Brahimi report, FN. 240, p. x

445 See e.g. *Mark Malan*, Physical Protection in practice: International and regional peacekeeping in Africa, African Security Review Vol. 9 No. 2 (2000).

446 See e.g. Peace Support Operations, Allied Joint Publication-3.4.1 (2001), para. 0634.

spoilers and that military units must be capable of defending themselves, other mission components and the mission mandate.[447] As these interventions have been based on current Security Council mandates, the development of requirements does not necessarily shift principle or legal background, but effectively implements existing approaches that might have been taken only with the knowledge that effective implementation will not take place.

With a view to the importance of the first twelve weeks following a ceasefire or peace accord it has been argued elsewhere that the United Nations must be able to deploy complex peace operations within 90 days of the adoption of the Security Council resolution.[448] In any case, effective and rapid deployment of peace operations would limit the period during which intervening forces must remain without any substantive backup. A gradual phase out would limit the commitment and the risks for the governments involved and might increase their willingness to participate in intervention activities.

Experience has shown that existing standby arrangements are dependent on the will of Member States to commit troops and equipment and, thus, do not provide a solution for the challenges.[449] Numerous attempts have been undertaken to provide the United Nations with the capacity to deploy quickly.

However, previous experience offers valuable entry points for further considerations, such as the conclusion that determined and selective deterrent operations targeting confirmed arms caches and individuals known to have illegal weapons in their possession could have prevented the genocide in Rwanda three month before it started.[450] Furthermore, guard tasks in the capital as a temporary measure had been employed. With a view to the main motives for committing genocide or large-scale human rights violations, the experience in Rwanda of the need to protect effectively the residences of key personalities and political actors from attacks will be among the tasks for military operations in the future.[451] With regard to the required size of an intervention force, it may be recalled that 2,500 soldiers had been considered to be able to limit massacres of the kind which began after the plane crash in Kigali.[452] In most cases of genocide and large-scale violations of human rights and humanitarian law, there are certain recurrent pattern in committing such crimes – road blocks in Rwanda, attacks on villages in Darfur – which could be influenced through tactical operation.

In addition, the proposal of intervention would be more acceptable to the Security Council, if it was presented with a clear and comprehensive assessment of the tasks, its relationship to international law, protection of civilians and other thematic concerns of the Council, and include an exit strategy. Member States are mainly

447 Brahimi report, FN. 240, p. X.
448 Op. cit., para. 86 et seq.
449 Rwanda report, FN. 259, p. 44.
450 Op. cit., p. 13.
451 Op. cit., p. 16
452 Op. cit., p. 30.

concerned at the protection of their troops participating in United Nations operations rather than the protection of the civilian population in the country concerned.

D. Conclusion

Under the leadership of the Secretary-General, United Nations departments, funds and agencies can take immediate steps towards the implementation of the agreement on the responsibility to protect in the Summit Outcome document. While an agreement in abstract between Member States on the relationship of sovereignty and the use of force, on criteria for a decision on the use of military force or on the legal character of the responsibility to protect will be difficult to find in the prevailing climate of international relations, the United Nations can begin its 'homework' of reviewing and developing a tool-box of measures tailored specifically at the prevention or halting of genocide, war crimes, crimes against humanity and ethnic cleansing. The agreement on the responsibility to protect will only add value to previous and ongoing initiatives to improve collective security for the benefit of individual rights-holders, if military intervention became a viable political option in these circumstances. To this end, the United Nations should explore options to cooperate with Member States and regional organizations in the development of doctrine for military operations limited to the protection of vulnerable groups which could fall victim to imminent or ongoing genocide, war crimes or crimes against humanity. The availability of practical tools will support unity among Member States to apply the responsibility to protect on a case-by-case basis. However, the responsibility to protect will only create this unity, if it was based on a common ethic, deriving from the United Nations Charter, which is applied by the Secretary-General to all Member States in all regional groups.

While the Secretary-General should exercise strong and visible leadership, the Special Adviser, who focuses primarily on the responsibility to protect, should coordinate the process of developing the toolbox and explaining the process to the Member States. The Special Adviser on the Prevention of Genocide should address county situations under his mandate by applying a continuum of measures from the toolbox in order to establish precedent cases and practical experience.

Bibliography

Abramovitz, Morton/ Pickering, Thomas, Making intervention work, Foreign Affairs, Vol. 87 (2008), No. 5, p. 100 et seq.

Acharya, Amitav, Redefining the Dilemmas of Humanitarian Intervention, Australian Journal of International Affairs, No.56, 2002, p.373 et seq.

Akhavan, Payam, Beyond Impunity: Can International Criminal Justice Prevent Future Atrocities?, AJIL Vol. 95, 2001, p. 7 et seq.

Annan, Kofi, Two Concepts of Sovereignty, Address to the 54th Session of the General Assembly, in: *United Nations* (ed.), The Question of Intervention: Statements by the Secretary-General of the United Nations Kofi Annan, New York, 1999, p. 39 et seq.

Badder, Ivo/ Goldgeier, James, Global NATO, Foreign Affairs, Vol. 85, 2006, Nr. 5, p. 105 et seq.

Banton, Michael, International Action Against Racial Discrimination, Oxford, 1996.

Barton, Frederick/ Hippel, Karen von Early Warning? A Review of Conflict Prediction Models and Systems, PCR Special Project Briefing, Center for Strategic and International Studies, February 2008.

Bass, Gory J., Freedoms Battle: The Origins of Humanitarian Intervention, London, 2008.

Beach, Hugh, Just War and the Responsibility to Protect: Developments in UN Peacekeeping and Humanitarian Intervention, Disarmament Diplomacy, Issue No. 80, 2005.

Bellamy, Alex, Whither the Responsibility to Protect? Humanitarian Intervention and the 2005 World Summit, Ethics and International Affairs, Vol. 20, 2006, p. 151 et seq.

Bettati, Mario/ Kouchner, Bernard (eds.), Le devoir d'ingerence, Paris, 1987.

Biersteker, Thomas J., Prospects for the UN Peacebuilding Commission, Disarmament Forum, 2007, no. 2, p. 37 et seq.

Birikorang, Emma, Operationalizing the "Responsibility to Protect", available at http://www.apsta-africa.org/news/article02032007.php

Brownlie, Ian, Principles of Public International Law, Fifth Edition, Oxford University Press, 1998, p. 293 et seq.

Chesterman, Simon, Just War or Just Peace: Humanitarian intervention and international law, Oxford University Press, 2001.

Cilliers, Jakkie, The African Standby Force: An Update on Progress, ISS Paper 160, 2008.

Crawford, James, The International Law Commission's Articles on State Responsibility: Introduction, Text and Commentaries, Cambridge University Press, 2002.

Dallaire, Romeo, Shake Hands with the Devil: The Failure of Humanity in Rwanda, Canada, 2003.

de Waal, Alex (ed.), War in Darfur and the Search for Peace, 2007.

de Waal, Alex, No Such Thing as Humanitarian Intervention. Why We Need to Rethink How to Realize the 'Responsibility to Protect' in Wartime, The Harvard International Review, 2008.

Deng, Francis M./ Kimaro, Sadikiel/ Lyons, Terrence /Rothchild, Donald/ William, I. (eds.), Sovereignty as Responsibility: Conflict Management in Africa, Washington, 1996.

Evans, Gareth, The Responsibility to Protect. Ending Mass Atrocity Crimes Once and For All, Brookings Institution Press, 2008.

Feil, Scott, Preventing Genocide: How the Early Use of Force Might Have Succeeded in Rwanda, Report to the Carnegie Commission on Preventing Deadly Conflict, April 1998.

Feinstein, Lee, Darfur and Beyond. What is Needed to Prevent Mass Atrocities, Council on Foreign Relations, 22 January 2007.

Ferencz, Benjamin, From Nuremberg to Rome: A Personal Account, in: *Mark Lattimer/ Philippe Sands* (eds.), Justice for Crimes against Humanity, Oxford, 2003, p. 31 et seq.

Flint, Julie/ de Waal, Alex, Darfur: A Short History of a Long War, 2006.

Fowler, Michael/ Bunck, Julie Marie, Law, Power, and the Sovereign State: The Evolution and Application of the Concept of Sovereignty, Penn State Press, 1995.

Fröhlich, Manuel, Political Ethics and the United Nations. Dag Hammarskjöld as Secretary-General, London, 2008.

Goulding, Marrack, The Evolution of United Nations Peacekeeping, International Affairs, Vol. 69, 1993, p. 451 et seq.

Gowan, Richard, EUFOR RD Congo, UNIFIL and future European Support to the UN, in: *SDA Discussion Paper*, The AU's Africa Strategy: What are the lessons of the Congo Mission?, Brussels, 2007, p. 29 et seq.

Groves, Steven, The U.S. Should Reject the U.N. 'Responsibility to Protect' Doctrine, Backgrounder No. 2130, 1 May 2008.

Gutman, Roy / Rief, David (eds.), Crimes of War. What the Public Should Know, New York, 1999.

Hamburg, David, Preventing Genocide: Practical Steps Toward Early Detection and Effective Action, Paradigm Publishers, 2008.

Harff, Barbara, No Lessons Learned from the Holocaust? Assessing Risks of Genocide and Political Mass Murder since 1955, American Political Science Review, Vol. 97, 2003, p. 57 et seq.

Hawk, David/ U.S. Committee for Human Rights in North Korea, The Hidden Gulag. Exposing North Korea's Prison Camps, 2003.

Henckaerts, Jean-Marie / Doswald-Beck, Louise, Customary International Humanitarian Law, Cambridge, 2005.

Holt, Victoria, The military and civilian protection: developing roles and capacities, HPG Report 21, p. 53 et seq.

Holt, Victoria/ Berkman, Tobias, The Impossible Mandate? Military Preparedness, the Responsibility to Protect and Modern Peace Operations, The Henry L. Stimson Center, 2006.

Holt, Victoria/ Shanahan, Maria, African Capacity-Building for Peace Operations: UN collaboration with the African Union and ECOWAS, Washington D.C., 2005.

Homan, Kees, Operation Artemis in the Democratic Republic of the Congo, in: *European Commission* (ed.), Faster and more united? The debate about Europe's crisis response capacity, May 2007, p. 151 et seq.

Human Rights Center, University of California, Berkeley, The Responsibility to Protect (R2P): Moving the Campaign Forward, 2007.

Human Security Center, Human Security Report 2005. War and Peace in the 21st Century, University of British Colombia, Canada, 2005.

ICISS, The Responsibility to Protect, Ottawa, 2002.

ICISS, The Responsibility to Protect. Research, Bibliography, Background, Ottawa, 2002.

Independent International Commission on Kosovo, Kosovo Report, Oxford, 2000.

Kelly, Ninette, International Refugee Protection Challenges and Opportunities, International Journal of Refugee Law, Vol. 19, No. 3, 2007, p. 401 et seq.

Khobe, Mitikishe Maxwell, The Evolution and Conduct of ECOMOG Operations in West Africa, ISS Monograph No. 44: Boundaries of Peace Support Operations, 2000.

Koops, Joachim/ Varwick, Johannes, Ten Years of SHIRBRIG, GPPi Research Paper Series No. 11 (2008).

Küng, Hans, Projekt Weltethos, München, 1990.

La Rosa, Anne-Marie, Humanitarian organizations and international criminal tribunals, or trying to square the circle, International Review of the Red Cross, Vol. 88, 2006, p. 169 et seq.

Lange, Maria/ Quinn, Mick, Meeting the Challenges, International Alert, December 2003.

Large, Judy, The War Next Door: A Study of Second-Track Interventions During the War in Ex-Yugoslavia, 1997.

Lemkin, Raphael, Genocide, American Scholar, Volume 15, no. 2 (April 1946), p. 227 et seq.

Luck, Edward C., The United Nations and the Responsibility to Protect, in: *The Stanley Foundation* (ed.), Policy Analysis Brief, August 2008.

MacFarlane, Neil/ Yuen Foong Khong, Human Security and the UN: A Critical History, Indiana University Press, 2006.

Mahoney, Liam, Proactive Presence. Field Strategies for civilian protection, Centre for Humanitarian Dialogue, 2006.

Malan, Mark, Physical Protection in practice: International and regional peacekeeping in Africa, African Security Review Vol. 9 No. 2 (2000).

Maundi, Mohammed Omar, Preventing Conflict Escalation in Burundi, in: *Chandra Lekha Sriram/ Karin Wermester* (eds.), From Promise to Practice. Strengthening UN Capacities for the Prevention of Violent Conflict (2003), p. 327 et seq.

Maybee, Larry/ Chakka, Benarji, Custom as Source of International Humanitarian Law, ICRC New Delhi, 2006.

Mendez, Juan E., Possibilities for Genocide Prevention, in: *Agnes van Ardenne – van der Hoeven/ Mohammad Salih/ Nick Grono* (eds.), Explaining Darfur: Four Lectures on the Ongoing Genocide, Amsterdam (2007), p. 49 et seq.

Mephan, David/ Ransbotham, Alexander Safeguarding Civilians. Delivering on the Responsibility to Protect in Africa, IPPR Report, 2007.

Metzl, Jamie, Rwandan Genocide and the International Law of Radio Jamming, AJIL, Vol. 91, 1997, p. 628 et seq.

Murhiti, Tim, The responsibility to protect, as enshrined in article 4 of the Constitutive Act of the African Union, African Security Review 16.2, p. 15.

Myint-U, Thant/ Busch, Sofia, Knowledge Needs at the UN Secretariat in the Field of Peace and Security: Reflections from 'The Knowledge Project', 2004.

Novosseloff, Alexanra, EU-UN Partnership in Crisis Management. Developments and Prospects, New York, 2004.

Peterson, Michael, The UN General Assembly, Routledge, 2006.

Physicians for Human Rights, Darfur – Assault on Survival. A Call for Security, Justice and Restitution, 2006.

Ponzio, Richard, The United Nations Peacebuilding Commission: origins and initial practice, Disarmament Forum 2007, no. 2, p. 5 et seq.

Prunier, Gerard, Darfur: The Ambiguous Genocide, Cornell University Press, Ithaca, 2005.

Ramcharan, Bertrand G., Early-Warning at the United Nations: the First Experiment. International Journal of Refugee Law, Vol. 1, 1989, p. 379 et seq.

Schabas, William A., An Introduction to the International Criminal Court, Second Edition, Cambridge University Press, 2004.

Schabas, William A., Genocide in International Law, Cambridge University Press, 2000.

Schorlemer, Sabine von, The Responsibility to Protect as an Element of Peace. Recommendations for its Operationalization, Development and Peace Foundation, Policy Paper 28, 2007, p. 5 et seq.

Seibert-Fohr, Anja, Reconstruction through Accountability, in: *Armin von Bogdandy/ Rüdiger Wolfrum* (eds.), Max Planck Yearbook of United Nations Law, Volume 9, 2005, p. 555 et seq.

Simma, Bruno, The Charter of the United Nations, 2nd ed., Oxford University Press, 2002

Slim, Hugo/ Eguren, Luis Enrique, Humanitarian Protection, A Guidance Booklet.

Slim, Hugo/ Mancini-Griffoli, Deborah, Interpreting Violence, Anti-civilian thinking and practice and how to argue against it more effectively, Centre for Humanitarian Dialogue, Geneva, 2008.

Smith, Joshua G., The Responsibility to Reflect: Learning Lessons from Past Humanitarian Military Interventions, Georgetown University, 2004.

Sokalski, Henryk, An Ounce of Prevention. Macedonia and the UN Experience in Preventive Diplomacy, United States Institute for Peace, 2003.

Srinivasan, Sharat Minority Rights, Early Warning and Conflict Prevention: Lessons Learnt from Darfur, Minority Rights Group, 2006.

Stahn, Carsten, Responsibility to Protect: Political Rhetoric or Emerging Legal Norm?, AJIL, Vol. 101, No. 1, p. 99 et seq.

Staudinger, Roland, Rassenrecht und Rassenstaat: Die nationalsozialistische Version eines "biologischen totalen Staates", 1999.

Tardy, Thierry, EU-UN cooperation in Peacekeeping: A Promising Relationship in a Constrained Environment, in: *Martin Ortega* (ed.), The European Union and the United Nations, Chaillot Paper 78, Paris, 2005, p. 49 et seq.

Task Force on the United Nations, American Interests and UN Reform, United States Institute for Peace, Washington D.C., 2005, p. 27 et seq.

United Nations (ed.), The Blue Helmets. A Review of United Nations Peace-keeping, Second edition, 1990.

United Nations Development Programme, Human Development Report 1994. New Dimensions of Human Security, Oxford University Press, 1994.

Wadlow, Rene, Darfur: The Responsibility to Protect, Newropeans Magazine, 2 April 2007.

Walter Dorn, Intelligence at UN Headquarters? Intelligence and National Security, Vol. 20, 2005, p. 440 et seq.

Winkelmann, Ingo, "Responsibility to Protect": Die Verantwortung der Internationalen Gemeinschaft zur Gewährung von Schutz, in: *Pierre-Marie Dupuy et al.* (eds.), Völkerrecht als Wertordnung, Kehl, 2006, p. 449 et seq.

Woocher, Lawrence, Early Warning for the Prevention of Genocide and Mass Atrocities, Paper presented at the annual meeting of the International Studies Association 48th Annual Convention, Chicago, 28 February 2007.

Xue, Hanquin, Chinese Observations on International Law. Speech at the International Criminal Law Network (ICLN), The Hague, 1 November 2006, available at http://www.icln.net